To My Family,
Irwin G. Spiesman
and Guy Dwight

CONTENTS

FOREWORD

To state the task facing the voter in many parts of the United States is sufficient to show why some parts of the American democratic machinery are creaking. To expect a voter to go into an uncomfortable polling booth and exercise from thirty to sixty choices in an intelligent manner in the few minutes allowed to him is highly unreasonable. The sources of information available to the voter are not equal to the task. It is not reasonable to expect the ordinary citizen to devote the time necessary to master the details even if the information were available. Psychologists and publicists have pointed out for many years that the voters are capable of exercising only the most general choices.

In the United States the choosing of many administrative officials by popular election has been made more objectionable because of the small size of most of the election districts. In the rapidly expanding urban communities, the multiplication of incorporated places and special districts has meant that the government of the entire region has been greatly handicapped. The immediate interests of the small suburban areas may run counter to the interests of the larger community. The smaller areas are unwilling to assume obligations which are theirs as a part of the larger community. Nowhere in the United States than in Chicago is it truer that local self-government for hundreds of tiny areas has meant the defeat of self-government for the larger community which is based on the identity of economic and social values.

The proposition is advanced that the larger the electoral unit, the greater are the chances of serving the interests of the largest possible number. In trying to apply this principle, one runs into another series of problems, namely, that the larger the electoral unit, the greater are the technical problems in running an election. This is most clearly illustrated in American national presidential elections where an elaborate system of presidential preference primaries and nominating conventions has still left unsolved some of the fundamental problems of representative democracy. The conventions have repeatedly defied the popular will as expressed in the preference primaries.

In making his choices, the present-day voter has to rely upon newspapers, political parties, civic organizations, local improvement associations, business associations, trade unions, friends and personal impressions obtained through such media as the radio, the newsreel, the platform, and face-to-face contacts. This volume is largely concerned with the face-to-face contacts.

A political party advertises its candidate by means of mass meetings, radio broadcasts, literature, and telephone and house-to-house calls. The information furnished by the political parties is one-sided in character. It is designed to inspire the faithful rather than to inform the doubtful or wavering.

The arguments presented by the party workers in going from house to house are not usually rational. Dr. Forthal in this volume has well established the thesis that many party workers appeal for votes not on the basis of the merits of their party candidates but on the basis of sympathy for themselves or the potential services which their party may render locally. She has shown how common was the "bread and butter" argument in Chicago politics of two decades ago. The tragedy of our democracy is that indifferent citizens without strong political convictions may be influenced by such arguments. These votes furnished the foundations of some of the so-called party "machines."

However, while the voters are sometimes influenced by non-rational factors, in the long run they show powers of discrimination. In the period described in this volume the late William Hale Thompson, mayor of Chicago, won votes by bizarre methods. He would campaign with a halter, a donkey, a burro, a horse, and a cage of rats. On the other hand, when his administration faced the serious problems of relief and unemployment in the depression which started in 1929, the voters turned to a more serious candidate.

In democratic jurisdictions where the parties are unbalanced or corrupt, where the press and radio are biased, it is still possible for citizens who have the common interest at heart to organize non-partisan civic groups to obtain and disseminate the truth about candidates and their policies. In the United States an outstanding organization of this type is the League of Women Voters which has more than a quarter century behind it of constructive political effort. The League may have its faults but as a democratic device for keeping the voters informed it stands as a monument of civic accomplishment that has withstood the storms of selfish partisan endeavors. Its chief weakness is the selected character of its membership. Its strength is least where it is most needed, in the poorer residential areas. In this volume, Dr. Forthal shows that it is not a necessary fault. There was no part of the city in the days of Al Capone that was too tough or dangerous for her to investigate.

Many things have happened since the materials for this volume were collected. When "Big Bill" Thompson died, a small fortune in cash was discovered in his safety deposit box. Following party changes in national, State and local elections, the political behavior of the Chicago Black Belt was completely altered.

COGWHEELS OF DEMOCRACY

Under the New Deal organized labor has acquired considerably more influence in local and national politics. In 1944 the Political Action Committee of the Congress of Industrial Organizations had its local political organization. In spite of all these changes, the need for personal contacts in political campaigning remains. In their classic study of the 1940 presidential campaign in an Ohio community, Messrs. Lazarsfelt and Berelson, and Miss Gaudet, admit that at another time they would place more stress on the local campaign and the role of face-to-face contacts. It is these contacts which are emphasized in the present volume. This work is an addition to a growing body of knowledge regarding local political behavior to which Salter, Kurtzman, Mosher, Peel, Reynolds, McKean, Weaver and others have made contributions.

HAROLD F. GOSNELL

Department of Political Science
University of Chicago

PREFACE

FAITH IN DEMOCRACY has too often tended to obscure certain defects in its functioning. The domination of political action by pressure groups, the frequent indifference of the electorate, and the corrupt practices accompanying elections are well known. It is a postulate of American democracy that a large proportion of the electorate is represented through candidates chosen and issues formulated by the two major parties. These parties function through political organizations which control the election machinery. Is the delegation of power to the political machines justified by the results? To determine an answer, this study is focused on the smallest agent of the machine—the precinct captain.

In the following pages, an attempt has been made to analyze the activities and characteristics of the precinct captain from interviews with six hundred of his kind taken from every ward of Chicago. His activities are contrasted with those of other community agents, such as the social worker or the policeman. Attention is given to his part in the election machinery, to his effectiveness as an interpreter and manipulator of local governmental functions, and to his role as a party agent.

Although the interviews upon which this study is based were made several years ago, the duties and responsibilities of the precinct captain have not changed. It is within the particularly notorious period of the "Pineapple Primary" of April, 1927, and the November election which chose "Big Bill Thompson" as mayor, that the precinct captains of the succeeding pages were most active.

Some precinct captains were not easy to find, and information about others was not readily procurable. The captain's "hangout" varied. He might be at home or in a dignified hotel room;

sometimes he was found in a flophouse or at the police station; he might be at the ward headquarters, in a garage, or in the neighborhood speakeasy. Wherever possible, the information obtained was verified by interviews with ward committeemen or secretaries, or with the precinct captains of the opposing faction or party in the same locality.

The succeeding chapters contain a description of the party system and the local political *milieu* of Chicago. Twenty-five selected cases and an analysis of the common characteristics of the 600 precinct captains give a composite picture of party organization and propaganda in the precincts.

In order to make this survey, the writer found it necessary to gain the cooperation of the persons in charge of the public and private social service agencies in Chicago, and of the officials concerned with the election machinery of the city. She interviewed many of the ward committeemen and aldermen, as well as the 600 precinct captains who answered the lengthy questionnaire described in the following pages. The writer wishes to express acknowledgment to all of these individuals.

For guidance in accumulating the facts contained in this study, the writer expresses her appreciation to Professors Charles E. Merriam, Harold F. Gosnell, and Robert Morse Lovett, of the University of Chicago. She also gives grateful acknowledgment to Professors Ernest Griffith and Catheryn Seckler-Hudson, of the American University, and to Constance Wagner. She acknowledges permission by the *Social Service Review* and the *American Political Science Review* for the use of the material each published. The field work for this study was made possible by a grant of the Local Community Research Committee of the University of Chicago. The more detailed annotated study may be found in the Library of the American University.

S. F.

COGWHEELS OF DEMOCRACY

1. PARTY PATTERNS: CHICAGO

Both of the major political parties function through a hierarchy of committees responsible for progressively smaller units: national, state central or executive, congressional, senatorial, county, city, and township or town. In the larger cities, the city committee functions through ward and precinct committees, the latter often consisting of one person, the precinct captain. Party leaders, bosses, and workers who may not belong to any committees also figure largely in politics.

All committees are charged with the management of party affairs in their geographical areas. Their power as directing agencies is often more formal than real, for the word of command most frequently comes from some individual on the outside who has come to be recognized as the party leader. Nor are these committees dependent upon each other, except insofar as they have the common interest of winning elections for their party, and insofar as they share campaign funds and patronage.

The local committees are influenced only indirectly by the national organization. The composition, function, and responsibility of the committees in the hierarchy have time and again been presented by writers on the subject. The precinct captain is immediately concerned only with city, ward, and precinct committees. He is on the job in every election—congressional, senatorial, city, and ward—but is accountable only to the ward committeeman, who in turn is responsible to the city boss.

It was certainly true in Chicago in the 1920's that the city committees of the Democratic Party and of the two main factions of the Republican Party coordinated the political work of the wards and acted as the machine of the urban political bosses. Then and since, each city committee embraces the ward committeeman from every ward, fifty in all. This committee has one purpose—to get as many people as possible to vote its party ticket. Before campaigns it provides local speakers, arranges through its precinct agents to distribute literature, and resorts to every known artifice to bring the voter to the polls on primary and election days. Moreover it is a dispenser of patronage and jobs.

The ward committeeman is nominated by petition of at least ten voters belonging to his faction, and usually by as many more as he can secure. A plurality of the votes in the ensuing primary elects the ward committeeman for a term of four years. A survey of the ward committeemen makes it clear that a basic qualification for the job is ability to gain sufficient patronage.

The ward committeeman is not paid by the party, but is usually an office-holder. A review of the 150 committeemen representing the two Republican factions and the Democratic Party in Chicago showed that 80 per cent derived a livelihood directly from politics, either as elected or appointed office-holders. The positions they held depended upon the patronage of their party.

The legal duties of the ward committeeman are varied. He is a delegate to the county convention which nominates candidates for the Circuit and Superior court benches and selects the delegates to the district convention, where a candidate for the State Supreme Court bench is chosen. He picks representatives from his ward to attend the state convention which nominates candidates for presidential electors and trustees of the state university, adopts the state platform, chooses members and alternates-at-large to the national convention, and fills vacancies. Above all, the ward committeeman is the representative of the locality in which he lives. The Ward Committeemen in Chicago correspond with the Precinct Committeemen in the unit voting areas outside the city; their legal duties are the same. They both differ from the precinct captain functioning in the smallest voting areas of the city whose party post is appointive. He serves on the city committee of his faction or party. As boss of the ward, he has the important function of picking the precinct captains and supplying them with political jobs. "I got most of my 31 precinct captains jobs," said one ward committeeman.

Great care is exercised in the choice of precinct captains; sometimes special inducements are offered even to the tried official in another party. This official is rated by the number of votes he controls in the primary election. The relation of the ward committeeman to the precinct captain is determined individually, within the tactical policies of the party. In the well-disciplined political machine, the ward committeeman is boss of the area, and the precinct captain does his bidding.

In Chicago, the precinct committee consists of one man, the captain, who may or may not have a number of lieutenants, or "heelers." He is responsible for a unit voting area, in which all the voters cast their ballots at a single polling place. The City Election Law provides that there shall be, as nearly as practicable, from four to six hundred qualified voters in a precinct. Each political party or faction is organized on this basis, and when completely organized, has a captain in each precinct.

The Chicago factions and parties during this period were not fully mannned to cover the entire city. They boasted an army of about 7,000 precinct captains. The Democratic Party and the Thompson Republicans had together approximately 5,000 captains, not counting the assistant captains and helpers; the Deneen

Republicans and all other lesser factions, such as the remnants of the Lundin-Small and Brundage partisans, about 2,000. More accurate figures are not procurable. The number of these officials in Chicago varies with the increase in population and the consequent redistribution of wards and precincts, with the intensity of the campaign, and with the extent of factionalism in the political parties.

The outstanding characteristics of the party system in Chicago during the first third of the twentieth century were the record of vehement factional warfare in the Republican Party, and the bi-partisan alignments of various Republican factions with the Democratic Party. Although factionalism covers mainly the activities of the political chiefs, it must include the man at the lowest rung of the political ladder, too.

Since shifts in factions mean shifts in power, patronage, and spoils, the entire political hierarchy is influenced through these changing patterns of job disposal. The precinct captain is as interested in jobs and favors as the man at the top of the ladder. Frequently, too, the man at the top of the municipal party machine started his career as a precinct official, and the tricks he learned serve him in good stead when he has reached the top. Anton Cermak, the late mayor of Chicago, and target for the bullet aimed at Franklin Delano Roosevelt, served as a precinct captain.

Since the character of the precinct captain's activities is the same in the shifting alignments of party groups, his rewards may vary, but not the essential technique of his work. No matter how his faction or party aligns itself, his importance depends on the number of voters he is able to influence.

2. PRECINCT CAPTAINS: 25 CLOSE-UPS

TWELVE PRECINCT CAPTAINS WERE CHOSEN FROM EACH WARD in the city of Chicago, irrespective of party, faction, religious creed, or nationality. They represented every level of society. Twenty-five cases are presented: eight from first-class, eight from middle-class, and nine from lower-class residential areas. They were chosen at random, being distinguished only by the fact that they could be located by the interviewer, and were willing to co-operate to the extent of answering the questionnaire.

First-class Residential Areas

FIRST-CLASS residential areas are defined as those where a four-room apartment rented for $81 a month or more, where the educational level was largely that of high school or college graduates, and where the residents were mostly first- or second-generation Americans.

Case I: An astute, American-born lawyer, well-dressed, polished in manner. He had lived in his locality for twenty-five years; his home was comfortably and tastefully furnished. While his faction was in power, he was an assistant state's attorney. Located in a university neighborhood, he had little influence. His constituents scorned his offers to help; they occasionally asked for an adjustment of taxes or the "fixing" of a speed slip; a few druggists who found the prohibition law inconvenient appealed for his aid.

Case II: A Lutheran of Swedish parents, he was born in Chicago, studied law, and settled in the area where his wife had been reared. Holding no political job, he had been active in political work for twelve years because of his desire to "clean out Crowe's hoodlums," and to "save good government." He sometimes guided dissatisfied constituents to the Board of Review for a reconsideration of their tax bills, or made adjustments himself. He was much influenced by Frank Loesch, of the Chicago Crime Commission, in whose employ he had worked for 20 years. Upon Loesch's advice, he became a candidate for alderman and for state representative, and was defeated for both offices. His faction was in the minority; the opposite faction usually carried the precinct because many of its job-holders lived there.

Case III: Born in New York City of German-Jewish parents, he was brought to Chicago at the age of four. His formal education ended with the fourth grade. He had an air of self-satisfaction, of one who was "self-made and proud of the job." He was a Mason and an Odd Fellow. He had been owner of a restaurant; then he had served as deputy clerk for the Municipal Court. Although he had been in politics for 26 years, he had spent only the last 10 in his present locality, a "silk stocking district." When he first took the precinct captaincy for the Deneen faction, 90 per cent of his constituents were Democrats; he succeeded in converting the precinct into a majority stronghold for his faction. In order to intrench himself in his locality, he organized a "Fellowship Club," with membership costing $200. He and his wife canvassed the precinct regularly before elections. He had "fixed" tax bills or traffic tickets and had placed a civil engineer with the Commonwealth Edison Company. He declared the following qualities were essential to being a successful precinct captain: to tell the truth to constituents, to make no promise which could not be fulfilled, to have a sober and morally sound personality, and to be courteous.

Case IV: A pleasant looking woman of about 50, who had been born in Ohio of Quaker parents, and had attended country school. About ten years before, her husband had been stricken with paralysis, and the burden of support had fallen upon her. She rented out part of her home, but derived insufficient income from that source. For the last six years, she had engaged in political activities. Asked why, she replied with a smile, "To get some of the graft!" She canvassed her area before primaries and elections and organized the women into a Ladies' Club. The voters were too well-to-do to require social service, but they were not above seeking reductions in taxes; when she was able to help them, they sometimes gave her "token" fees. These, and her official election fees, constituted all the "graft" she received. When traffic violators were first offenders, she used her influence on their behalf to get the charge dropped, or the fine reduced. She admitted that she found it difficult to reconcile some of the activities of the Thompson Republican faction with her Quaker ideals; sometimes she wished she were out of politics altogether.

Case V: A Chicagoan by birth, with a German father, she was a tall, well-built woman, neatly dressed. Her father, a precinct captain, had helped her to get a political job with the Deneen Republicans. She had filled it for four years, and had a well-paid position as secretary to a Sanitary District trustee. Grateful to her faction for her job, she made a personal appeal to influential people to vote "her way." "Honesty, a clean character, aggressiveness, and affiliation with the right party," were regarded by her as desirable in a precinct captain.

Case VI: He came to Chicago from Norway at the age of 17; completed high school and a law course, and had lived in his precinct seven years. He had served as deputy coroner and was employed also as an abstract-maker in a banking house. His interest in politics dated back 25 years. He gained control in his district because he had political affiliations—with the Thompson Republican faction—and because, in a new community, the people needed guidance in land deals and in zoning problems. He was formerly superintendent of the Albany Park district. As father of six children, he saw the need of a park in his present area. He succeeded in getting one, which his neighbors named after him.

Case VII: A Chicagoan of Irish parentage, a university graduate, at one time assistant attorney general, this man represented a "gold coast" constituency, one third of whom were Jews, living mostly in luxurious apartments and hotels. He had been in political work for 27 years, 12 of them in his present precinct. His party affiliation—with the Thompson faction—and his law practice were mutually helpful; he gained a wide acquaintance and many clients; he knew the municipal judges whom he helped to elect. The routine techniques employed by many precinct captains were not effective in his locality—he found social and business clubs more useful. He belonged to the Edgewater Athletic Club, the Waveland Club, the Pleasure Club, the Seventh Regional Service Men's Association, and the Chicago Bar Association.

Case VIII: Forty-five years of age, a Democrat, the Chicago-born son of Russian-Jewish parents, this man had attended Northwestern University Law School for three years. He had held a number of political positions including those of special prosecutor for the federal government and special master in chancery for the federal District Court. For 17 years he had been ·n political work, having started as clerk of election in another precinct; he had lived six years in his present locality. His following was gained through his synagogue, his business contacts, and social clubs. In spite of the breadth of his experience, he was ill at ease when conversing, smoked incessantly, and talked vociferously. His constituents were well educated second- or third-generation Americans.

IT CAN be concluded that in the first-class residential areas, the successful precinct official possesses economic sufficiency, social homogeneity, and adequate educational advantage. Except in a few precincts where there were conscientious officials, the party organization operated largely through the number of jobs it had at its disposal, through the men with wide connections whom it found to represent it, and through social functions.

Middle-class Residential Areas

MIDDLE-CLASS residential areas are defined as those where the rental for a four-room apartment ranged from $51 to $80 a month; where the educational level of the constituents ranged from literates to high school graduates, and where the residents were chiefly first- or second-generation Americans, largely of Irish, German, Scandinavian, British, or Russian origin.

Case I: A tall, strapping Irish ice contractor, who boasted of his ardent Catholicism, he lived in an opulently furnished home in a building which he owned. He was a widower; one daughter stayed at home and acted as assistant precinct captain; the other was employed in the Law Department of the Board of Education; his two sons were in business. Certain members of the

[23]

Thompson faction had tried to lure him from the Democratic party, but in vain. He declared that he enjoyed serving his neighbors, and was not averse to "appreciation votes." Because he had successfully fought a movement to locate an incinerator plant in his district, his neighbors elected him park commissioner.

Case II: A native of Georgia, of Scotch descent, this man was a Protestant and a Republican. Through a friend he became interested in politics, and was given a political job. Before his appointment as clerk in the Municipal Court, he had worked as a sales executive and as private secretary. He was well known in his district—a personal letter from him was enough to send most of his friends to the polls. He fortified his interest by appointing his wife to act as judge of elections and by insisting that ballots be counted, not "weighed." Except for helping some persons to find employment on the Board of Review or in business houses, he performed no benevolent office. Faithful to the axiom that a politician must have many friends, he was cordial to everyone.

Case III: A woman (whose father had been a precinct captain for 15 years) and her husband. They worked together throughout the year, serving their friends and neighbors in countless ways. The wife was active in the Parent-Teacher Association and in neighborhood clubs. She visited the sick and the afflicted; many a story was told of her kindliness. The captain interceded for his constituents when they wished to have taxes adjusted or "slips fixed." Before primaries and elections, he canvassed his precinct diligently, reminding his neighbors of past favors and impressing upon them the merits of his cause. Both husband and wife helped to round up indifferent voters; they also presided over the opening, sorting, and counting of votes. They knew that success in politics depends largely upon "knowing the ropes" and keeping friendships in repair.

Case IV: Another husband-wife arrangement. The husband was a Democratic state representative; his wife was a precinct captain in the district which he represented. Until his wife encouraged him to study law, he had been employed as an advertising salesman. He had lived in his district for 12 years; for 20, he had been interested in politics. As representative, he never made a promise he could not fulfill. He had been especially active in securing medical care and hospitalization in state institutions, and in releasing law violators. Callers came frequently to his home to ask for favors ranging from tax adjustment to getting a job. Generosity and friendliness marked both the representative and his wife in all their dealings.

Case V: An active member of the Daughters of the American Revolution, this woman was proud that a distant relative had been among the signers of the Declaration of Independence, that her father was a Civil War veteran who had been commissioned by Abraham Lincoln, and that her brother had fought in the Spanish-American War. She regarded her membership in the Republican Party as a tribute to her father and her brother; she campaigned ardently for Thompson. She had been interested in politics ever since Illinois women first excised the ballot. Seven years ago the ward committeeman had asked her to move into her present locality. She had two complaints: it was difficult to get American-born women out to vote, and women precinct officials were paid less than half as much as the men, though they did most of the work. She had given up membership in various clubs in order to be able to devote all her energies to her political work.

[25]

Case VI: A second-generation Chicagoan, a Democrat and Catholic, this man had been engaged in political work for 34 years. Leaving high school after the second year, he had studied engineering. He was a county supervisor and ward committeeman as well as precinct captain, and had other party responsibilities. His position on the County Board made it possible for him to help some of the needy members of his party and their friends. He attributed to Mayor Harrison II his belief that success in politics depended upon hard work, a friendly personality, a wide acquaintanceship, and painstaking canvassing at regular intervals.

Case VII: Living in a distinguished looking apartment house in a middle-class Negro neighborhood, himself a native of Vicksburg, Mississippi, this Negro was a representative of the Thompson faction. His interest in politics had begun 18 years before, but he had lived in this precinct only two years. Speaking clear, correct English, with no trace of Southern accent, he was prepared at any time to set forth the glories of the Republican Party, which he regarded as the greatest of all political institutions. Most of the benevolent offices in his district were performed by the ward committeeman or by the county treasurer; he himself held a job as a city employee.

Case VIII: Assistant director of the County Public Welfare Bureau, "lady ward committeeman" for the Democratic Party, active member or seven social or benevolent clubs, mother and grandmother, this precinct captain seldom found time hanging heavy on her hands. Born in Chicago, she had completed secondary school and then married. For 14 years she had been an active party worker; whenever social service was sought by other members of her organization, she was the one through whose efforts the needs were met. The Chief of the Service recommended her as an efficient and diligent public executive.

IT WAS observed that in the middle-class areas the precinct captain is more nearly typical of the locality than in the better residential areas. His educational and social status reflects that of his constituents. The most distinguishing difference is that politics is not a side interest, but a profession.

Lower-class Residential Areas

LOWER-CLASS residential areas are defined as those where the rental for a four-room apartment ranged from $10 to $50 a month, where the educational level of the constituents seldom went above that of the grade school and not a few had had no schooling at all, and where many were of foreign birth.

Case I: Born in New York City, of Russian-Jewish parents, this man married a woman who was born in London; they had a seven-year-old son. She had been interested in politics before her husband, and had urged him to make a career of it. Energetic, ambitious, and unscrupulous, she carried on most of the organization, propaganda, and social activities connected with the work, leaving him free to devote his time to two jobs—one as a license investigator for the city, and the other with a candy concern. A Deneen Republican first paid her $25 to canvass the district. Later, when her husband lost his job, a Thompson ward committeeman gave him a salary without a job on condition that he join the Thompson faction. The precinct was a strategic one; in the 1927 mayoralty election, the Thompson faction won by only five votes. His wife guarded the interests of her faction so closely on election day that she engaged in malpractice which eventually brought her to trial.

Case II: Having come from Poland at the age of 18, this man had lived in Chicago for 17 years. His first political affiliation was with the Democratic Party. Six years before, he had come over to the Republicans, and was now one of the few Catholics connected with the Deneen faction. He had a genial manner and a warm smile. The fact that he could scarcely read or write did not distinguish him from most of his constituents. He and his family lived in the rear of his shoe repair shop which was a social center for the community. He held no political job. His most common service was to release people who had been lodged in the police station for disorderly conduct or for "clothes-line fights."

Case III: Born in Chicago, of Irish parents, he left school at the end of the seventh grade, and went to work. During 21 years in politics, he became an important employee of the Board of Election Commissioners, and served in the office of the county treasurer and elsewhere. In order to increase the number of votes, he was active in obtaining the release of boys held for petty stealing. His acquaintance with many prominent politicians made him an influential friend to those in need; he was able to distribute jobs in the city's water, pipe, and street cleaning departments. He regarded no favor to a constituent as too insignificant to merit his interest.

Case IV: A Chicago-born Negro, whose father had come from Kentucky, this precinct captain was also bailiff in the Municipal Court. He had stopped going to school when he reached the fifth grade, but had tried to educate himself to some extent. Because of his political activities, he paid only nominal rent for his three-room apartment owned by the county treasurer, George Harding, close friend of Mayor Thompson. He was engaged in the cleaning and dyeing business. He organized a political, social, and civic club whose 80 members paid monthly dues of 10 cents each. Seven "stick-up men" were pledged to keep thieves and hold-up men out of the district, and had so far succeeded. He was a member of the Knights of Pythias and of the Elks; his wife belonged to a woman's club, the "Mysterious Ten." Most of his constituents had recently migrated from the South; they were illiterate or with very meager education.

Case V: Coming from Italy at the age of 13, this man had been in Chicago for 24 years; for the last eight, he had lived in the precinct. Unhampered by any trade or business of his own, he was dickering with rival politicians for a job which would pay him $300 a month instead of the $200 he was receiving. Being obliged to report daily irked him; he wanted a job which involved less drudgery. Whichever faction managed to get him such a job would receive his support. He was a busy errand-boy for his constituents, endeavoring to get taxes reduced, and expecting a portion of the amount saved, supplying bail for drunkenness and disorderly conduct cases, and paying fines for the expiration of automobile and truck licenses. He charged fees for among his trusty cohorts, and managed to get city pay-roll jobs most of these services. He had eight political jobs to distribute for several more.

Case VI: He had come to Chicago from Indiana 10 years ago, was a high school graduate, a Catholic, and a Deneen Republican—a somewhat unusual combination. Thirty-five years old, he was the father of four children. For three years, he had been active politically, beginning as election clerk. The fact that he was for a time the commander of his American Legion post contributed to his usefulness; many of the members lived in his area.

His services to his constituents were chiefly social and charitable. He canvassed his precinct diligently and regularly, and his faction carried the precinct.

Case VII: Himself of French and Italian parentage, this man was well qualified to manage a precinct in which only 180 out of 429 registered voters were American-born. Catholic, a Democrat, his formal education had ended with grammar school. He was married and had two children; his wife assisted him in his political work. Now 52 years of age, he had been a saloon-keeper until 1916. Becoming more and more interested in politics, he finally made it his chief business. He had held many a government and party job by the patronage of his party. He found money and jobs valuable in getting votes; on eleceion day he used as many workers as his purse permitted. He adjusted taxes for 50 or 60 persons a year; when he served in Judge X's court, he "fixed slips" by the armful. He contacted his constituents in as many ways as possible—at funerals, in times of trouble or illness, at Christmas time, on social occasions. He developed a faction which was interested primarily in doing his bidding, and only secondarily in party or candidate. Talkative and jovial, he greeted everyone as a friend. His fellow employees in the office of the Board of Election Commissioners regarded him as one of the best Democratic precinct captains in the city. He exemplified his idea that a precinct captain should know people, grant favors, and have a cheerful disposition.

Case VIII: Chicago-born, Catholic, a Thompson Republican, this man had established residence in a neglected rooming-house area whose inhabitants ranged from transients to a few exceedingly well-to-do persons who operated night clubs, "speakeasies," and sundry illicit activities. Attendance at the University of Minnesota led to a study of law, but the war interrupted this work. For seven years he had lived in this locality because he found it a political plum; his wife resided in a suburb. The high point of his services to his constituents had been to obtain a year's probation for two boys who were sentenced to the penitentiary for stealing; he had furnished many bonds; had protected a number of women, "guardians" of disorderly houses, and had secured the release of inebriates who were jailed for "disorderly conduct." With the assistance of two lawyers, members of his organization, he was ready at all times to furnish legal aid. Only after much persuasion did he admit that he was employed as inspector by the School Board. He hoped to be a state representative.

Case IX: Coming to Chicago from Germany 40 years ago at the age of 5, this woman, Catholic, and a Thompson Republican, had been left a widow with five small children. For a time she supported them by taking in washing; then she secured a job cleaning offices in the City Hall. She gradually advanced to a position as deputy bailiff. After serving as precinct captain for a time, she had a disagreement with the ward committeeman upon whose assistance she had largely depended, and lost not only the captaincy but, what was far worse, her appointment as deputy bailiff. The committeeman was all-powerful in this district; all social and benevolent activities were administered with his aid and approval. She was left with a reliable constituency, but no factional affiliation.

THE PRECINCT captains functioning in poor residential areas were as colorful as the nationalities they represented. Except for the lawyers, who were few, none of them had superior educational or cultural equipment; none of them was socially or economically far removed from the voters. This fact was one of their strongest assets. Whatever advantage they had over their constituents came to them through the political party and through their connections with governmental institutions.

CONCLUSION

THE OUTSTANDING characteristic of the precinct captain in each of the residential areas was his vocational interest. Politics in a vague way constituted his profession—a profession, however, that required no preparation and no specific qualifications other than the ability to get votes. Furthermore, his vocation was usually subsidized by an administrative task he performed in a governmental agency.

Aside from this common characteristic, the precinct captain cannot be classified as a type. Each captain corresponded to the constituency he served, was to an extent conditioned by it. The more successful possessed a bluff personality, a flair for politics, and above all, the professional capacity to seem to be everybody's friend, especially before a primary or an election, and to seem to serve the voter while serving himself.

The next chapter will attempt a summary of the characteristics found common to 600 precinct captains when measured statistically.

3. PRECINCT CAPTAINS: A GROUP PICTURE

THE OVERWHELMING MAJORITY OF THE SIX HUNDRED PRECINCT captains studied were native-born Americans of foreign stock. Their nationalities, the areas in which they lived, the occupations they pursued, and the social groups they formed were characteristic of the Chicago electorate.

The Italians, and those of recent Italian origin, had the highest pro-rata representation of precincts in this sample. Following them in order were Poles, English-Scotch-Welsh, old stock Americans, Russians (largely Jews), Irish, Norwegians, Austrians, Canadians, Czechoslovakians, Lithuanians, Swedes, and a miscellany of other nationalities found in the city.

About three quarters of these party officials were native-born Americans; of these, a majority were born in Chicago. A striking difference was apparent in the distribution of their fathers' birthplaces: only one-fourth of the fathers were American born: then followed those of German birth, 18 per cent; Irish, 17 per cent; and Poles, more than 8 per cent.

The local party functionaries settled largely in residential localities occupied by their own racial group. This was just as true of those whose parents were born in this country as of those who had recently arrived. The party officers having Italian, Polish, Negro, Czechoslovakian, and Jugoslavian fathers were found living mainly in the poor residential areas of the city. Those with Irish, German, and Russian fathers appeared most frequently in the middle-class areas, and those with American-born fathers were most often found in the more prosperous areas. Party agents of the various other nationalities were found also in the poor and middle-class localities. The few captains born in Norway and Lithuania lived exclusively in the middle-class areas. Only two of foreign birth were found in the first-class areas, and these represented localities other than those they lived in. Within each residential classification, the majority of the captains were native Americans, and more than half of them were native Chicagoans. The party machine functioning in Chicago precincts seemed to be controlled by native Americans

There was less illiteracy among these officials than among the voters they represented; there were among them, also, considerably more college and professional school graduates. However, more than half of them and the great majority of the voters in the Chicago area had gone no further than grammar school. The officials living in the poor areas were predominantly of grammar school training; those in the middle-class localities were usually high school graduates; those in the good residential districts usually had college or professional education.

Maturity and length of residence were outstanding characteristics of the party representatives in Chicago. The majority were men varying in age from 30 to 55. Of the 600 captains, 60 per cent of those in the poor and middle-class residential districts had lived in the same localities their entire lives. The majority of the captains had lived in the same precinct more than ten years; this span characterized all the captains, regardless of the economic status of the area in which they lived. Some had only "paper" residences, especially in the poor areas which were in a state of transition, and in the "gold coast" or first-class sections of the city. Generally, however, the captain lived in the locality he represented. When he lived elsewhere his helper or helpers lived within the precinct, and maintained direct contact with the voters.

The local dignitaries gave various reasons for choosing their locations. Choice of the locality in which a captain served might hinge on his being asked to take charge by the ward committee-man or alderman, on his being born in the locality, having friends or relatives living there, or finding the neighborhood atmosphere congenial. The captains in middle-class districts most often settled in a particular precinct because of ownership of property or because of a large acquaintanceship and the presence of many relatives. The influx of new racial groups, or the normal transition of areas from residential to business, was frequently responsible for a shift in residence, but were not as determining as the wishes of the party "machine."

The precinct captains came from poor or middle-class economic and social circles. The city's "better people" are apparently absorbed in other activities than those demanded of a precinct captain in a large urban community. Nor has the profession of politics reached a dignity sufficient to attract them. Although there is no salary connected with this position, their main interest in politics is economic. In this respect the precinct captain is no different from the man above him in the party hierarchy—the ward committeeman. The ward committeemen in Chicago are elected officials presumably functioning without compensation; actually, eighty per cent of them hold governmental jobs while they represent their wards.

An examination of the jobs held by the party officials studied showed that 70 per cent of them were engaged in governmental service. Of this group, 20 per cent of them were with the city, 17 per cent with the county, nearly 10 per cent with the Sanitary District, more than 9 per cent with the courts. Three per cent were elected to office and financially remunerated thereby; over 2 per cent were employed by the state, and less than 2 per cent by the federal government. Most of the political jobs held by the captains were not under civil service, but were distributed through party channels. Of the other occupations or industries pursued by them, the percentage distribution in order of frequency ran as follows: salesmen, investigators, superintendents, managers, and foremen, over 13 per cent; skilled and semi-skilled, nearly 10 per cent; the same percentage for clerical, office, stenographic, and telegraphic workers; nearly 7 per cent lawyers, less than 7 per cent in retail business; 6 per cent in miscellaneous occupations; about 5 per cent in professions other than law; more than 4 per cent were real estate operators, insurance agents, or stock brokers; more than 2 per cent worked in public utilities and transportation, 1 per cent in manufacturing, and less than 1 per cent in domestic services or unskilled labor.

When the occupations of the local party officers are compared with those pursued by the entire population, it is seen that an exceptionally large proportion of them were government employees and lawyers. In an urban community like Chicago where judges are elected to office, the implication is obvious. Many judges started as precinct captains, studied law, and eventually climbed to the bench via the political ladder.

Frequent judicial elections increased the need for judges to maintain their political contacts. Even when a lawyer was not concerned with becoming a judge, he was always interested in developing a clientele or in winning cases, and to this end he often found a reliable voting constituency and friends in the political party definite assets. Many of the assistant corporation counsels of the municipality and the trustees of the Sanitary District were precinct bosses. This was also true of the assistant state's attorneys.

The bosses of the precincts quite frankly admitted that they were active party agents because they expected economic reward. In fact, many acknowledged that failure in the economic world drove them to politics. One entered the political arena because his health failed. Another entered because of the seasonal variations in his trade; he had been unemployed for thirteen weeks when his alderman offered him a job if he would canvass the precinct. In another instance, the unit captain was engaged in seasonal employment, painting and decorating. By aligning himself with a contractor who worked for the city, he stabilized his trade and income. Politics and party affiliations helped one man out of the depths of despair. He had neither a trade nor money when he first became a local party representative; his family, a wife and two children, were living in a damp, dirty basement and relying upon the support of friends and relatives. The alderman offered him employment if he would bring votes. At the next aldermanic campaign he canvassed all his neighbors; he harassed them until they promised their votes. He carried his precinct, and was duly rewarded with a job in the Sanitary District. Later, when this official contracted tuberculosis, the party organization collected a fund large enough to send him to Denver. His name remained on the payroll, and his salary was collected by his wife. Injuries received in World War I disabled a former department store manager, and he turned to politics. Rheumatism caused a waiter to become a captain. According to one captain, "practically all precinct officials are jobholders . . . the only real interest is economic." Negro captains were especially attracted to politics for economic reasons; very few white-collar jobs were otherwise open to them. Of the 12 captains who had Negro constituencies, nine held political jobs, one owned property in the district, and another anticipated a job.

Party agents in the poor and middle-class areas of Chicago tended to become dependent upon their political jobs. The tasks they performed usually required so much time that they were unfitted for work at their own occupation. The jobs they were given in the various government departments were based on their party activities, even when these meant the neglect of their official duties. Fitness for governmental employment was rarely taken into consideration. Since in the main, the unit party official received his job through his party, his first interest was to please those who had secured the job for him. Even when selection for recruitment was made on the basis of a competitive examination, political bosses found innumerable loopholes for party intervention.

In a number of instances, especially in the city government, the party officials were given their posts without examination. If they took any examination, they usually did so after they were given their jobs, if members of the opposite party objected to their appointment. Often those who stood high on the civil service list were forced to waive their rights in favor of a party-picked applicant whose rating was much lower. The precinct captain in a government job was expected to perform two functions—one for his faction, and the other for the city or county. The Chicago taxpayer paid for the services he performed as a party agent.

The city appropriated $212,293,691.92 in 1927 for the maintenance of its governmental machinery. The budget did not include services rendered by the precinct captains to their political factions. Yet it has been shown that 70 per cent of the 600 were in government employ and that these positions were granted as rewards for party work. More than this, not only the appointment but the type of service and the amount of remuneration were conditioned by political patronage. Fifteen of the precinct officials stated that they were planning to sever their connections with their factions because promises made had not been fulfilled. In one striking instance, a precinct captain refused to report at the government office in which he was employed because he considered $200 a month inadequate pay.

Even though not holding governmental jobs, many of these

party men derived economic benefits from politics. This was true of those engaged in retail business in their localities, such as a restaurant, a drug-store, or a "speakeasy." Some merchants, however, refused to "mix business and politics." The corner druggists in the better neighborhoods who sold "prescriptions," found political connections helpful when a prohibition agent became bothersome. The "speakeasy" proprietor was constantly at the mercy of some political agent, from the policeman on his beat to the alderman. When he was vested with some political power, it was considerably to his advantage. The salesmen and insurance agents found politics useful—the more people they knew, the greater the possibility of selling their commodities. One salesman gained ready access to county and state institutions through his connections as a party worker and found that political pull helped to sell machinery. Property owners found that precinct work saved them many a penny in taxes. For the lawyer, a precinct captaincy was often the first step upon the political ladder. It was an opportunity to become personally acquainted with judges in the local courts, especially when a judge was the committeeman of the ward served by the captain. The captains who were engaged in the draying and trucking business found their political connections useful; their trucks were often used by the city. An ambitious Italian functionary earned his livelihood by making wine in his basement. He shifted his allegiance to the faction which furnished him the greatest protection. The owner of a cheap vaudeville theatre also found his political connections an asset to his business. A master plumber found that being a captain simplified some problems; a word from a fellow party-member, the building commissioner, made it unnecessary to redo work not in accordance with city regulations.

Although the economic motive was primary, this was not the only consideration which held the captain to his task. Friend-

[39]

ship for, or obligation to, a political personage, such as the alderman or the ward committeeman, was offered as a reason. A Negro official, holding a political job, spoke of the mayor as the "biggest man since Abraham Lincoln," and offered this belief as a reason for serving him. In local elections, the Negro vote was usually Republican. In this specific instance, the precinct captain's racial loyalty was reinforced by a job in the city administration. Frequently loyalty was based on a special favor. One captain who had been arrested following a saloon brawl, was released by the alderman. Later, the same captain, annoyed by a man who had "squealed and turned yellow," shot him in the leg. Again his political friend came to the rescue. These two deeds of kindness forever bound him to the alderman.

In another East Side precinct, a judge found employment for jobless voters and thereby bound them to his faction. Another judge, very active in politics, induced a young lawyer to "join the game" and offered him a job as bailiff. Two captains became active when they wished to elect their relatives to office.

The prestige value of political connections was also found to be a motive. The president of a synagogue was politically active because it enhanced his standing with his congregation. He attended political banquets and met prominent people. This established him as a man of wide contacts and added to his influence. Politics, to one captain, meant associations pleasing to his wife. To another captain, politics offered "excitement." Still another stated that his "instincts were kindled" when he heard men discuss politics. Political ambitions dominated many captains.

Desire for clean government and improvement of civic conditions motivated only a few. Nor was party loyalty a very vital factor. The sustaining interest was inevitably based on practical returns. A woman functionary admitted that she did not like her numerous official chores, but continued in order to get "some of the graft." Her "graft" was the job she held in the county administration.

There were some differences between the various localities. The poor man with limited opportunities living in a slum locality became an active worker to lighten his financial burden. He saw the ward committeeman looking prosperous while seemingly doing nothing, and wished to rise to the same heights. The captaincy was only a step toward better political plums. In middle-class and upper-class neighborhoods, the party representatives sometimes engaged in politics for the good fellowship and the "fight" associated with campaigns. For the most part, political machines functioned on the basis of practical emoluments and perquisites. One West Side ward committeeman, addressing his captains before a campaign, said, "You and I know what a political machine is: it's jobs and more jobs, and if you want to keep yours, you'd better come across with your precinct. The Central Committee expects me to carry the ward, and I expect you to land every voter in your precinct. Don't fool yourself; we know what work you are doing; you'll hear from us the day after........gets in."

Eighty per cent of the precinct captains interviewed were married men; nearly 60 per cent had children; a number of them had grandchildren. Only 10 per cent were unmarried; a scattering were widowed or divorced. The wives of most precinct captains living in poor and middle-class residential areas assisted them in the work of the bailiwick. In a number of instances, especially in the poorer sections, when the husbands were employed in government offices, the wives performed many of the minor political duties. Safeguarding their own family was their prime interest. The captain in some localities was often driven into corrupt political practices by the urgent economic needs of his family.

The home of the local dignitary varied with the locality in which he functioned. In the middle-class areas, his home closely resembled that of his neighbors; in the good residential areas, it was usually somewhat inferior.

Friendliness and a desire to cooperate were the predominating personal characteristics observed during the interviews, along with a certain cautiousness and suspicion, even extending to fear and evasiveness. Sincerity, forcefulness, loquacity, and humor declined in frequency. Qualities even more rarely found were cunning, ostentation, and self-satisfaction. A few were idealistic enough to believe they could clean up their political party by serving as captains; one woman captain limited her ideals to cleaning up the neighborhood. Some ignored their opponents; others denounced them. The captains in foreign areas invariably spoke the language of the locality as well as English. In the good residential areas, the precinct captains possessed poise, fluency, and a degree of pompousness. In all the areas, docility to the superior in the party hierarchy was an outstanding characteristic.

Each local party dignitary was asked to enumerate the qualities he regarded as essential for a successful party representative. In order of their frequency the answers were as follows: the capacity to do favors, "to have an ear for every one's troubles," the ability to make friends, cordiality, a degree of charitableness, salesmanship, personality, the ability to hustle and work hard, intelligence, and obedience to the "chief." In the more sophisticated neighborhoods, the qualities included dignity, respect, and making good all promises; this last attribute was also enumerated by the captains in the average and poor localities. Some practical qualities specified, especially in the poor areas, were the ability to canvass, to provide protection to the people in the precinct, and to manipulate the police. The ability to canvass and to satisfy all promises made were regarded as essential equipment in all the residential areas.

The views on politics enunciated were decidedly inchoate; very few were interested in theoretical speculations. To a number, politics was a "wonderful game"; "life is a game of politics, with one faction always fighting another." A Pole and a Negro found they could help their groups through politics. "Service is the watchword of politics." There are, for instance, more competent teachers than there are positions for them; the political organization helps such teachers find jobs—"That's not corruption, that's service," said another. "Justice is secured through party connections; without political friends you can't get justice in the courts of Chicago." Politics was also regarded as an opportunity to "rub elbows" with people. A few of the party stewards considered it their duty to be in politics. "Too many scoundrels run the game, and if a few clean-minded men would get into it, they could easily cleanse the government." To a highly conscientious captain, politics was a "dirty" game which needed cleansing. The remedy he suggested was to convert all spoils offices into appointive or elective ones. Only a few insisted that the political machinery of the city should be changed. For some of them politics was fascinating—"he who enters the political game finds it difficult to retire from it." Among the attractions of the game were included the element of campaign uncertainties, its sociabilities, and its conflicts. In general the theoretical conceptions held by the 600 captains were neither coherent nor original. They were usually a re-echo of the campaign slogans of their party bosses. Such obviously re-echoed cliches did not contribute many clues to the personality of the precinct captains.

About 5 per cent of the precinct captains interviewed were women; these were found specially in the middle-class and poor residential areas. They showed no significant differences in characteristics and activities from the men. In general, they held places subordinate to the male captain in the party hierarchy, and they "knew the ropes" less intimately. More than half were between the ages of 40 and 50; the rest were mostly younger. Clerical work was the occupation listed by more than a third of the group; housework by another third. Nearly one-fifth were city, county, or federal employees, and the remainder held miscellaneous jobs. Their motive was generally economic; in only two instances were the women imbued with idealistic motives. Both of these joined the less corrupt local faction to clean their neighborhoods and to oust the mayor from office.

An analysis of the precinct captains according to political faction or party showed only minor variations. The sample covered showed nearly 43 per cent Thompson Republicans, more than 39 per cent Democrats, and more than 17 per cent Deneen Republicans. A slightly higher per cent of the Thompson Republican precinct captains were found in the poorer residential areas. The educational background of the captains in the various factions and parties showed a remarkable similarity. The Deneen faction showed a slightly higher frequency of those with no formal education, the lowest frequency of those with professional training, and a slightly higher frequency of captains with high school and college training. The Democratic Party had a slight edge in the percentage of captains with grammar school background.

Differences in the religious affiliations of these officials were also slight. Captains of Protestant faith were found more frequently in the Deneen faction; the Catholics, in the Democratic Party. Jewish precinct captains were more common in the Democratic Party with the Thompson Republicans next. In the Deneen faction, only 8 per cent of the captains were Jews.

The occupations pursued by the precinct captains in the different factions were markedly similar.

DOES AN analysis of the data concerning the precinct captains make possible a composite picture having diagnostic value? Is there a typical precinct captain? Most emphatically not. The captains resemble their constituents in education and in economic and social status. Since they form a professional or occupational class, they are stamped by certain common traits, even in an unstandardized profession. The quality of friendliness appears with greatest frequency among the 600 precinct captains, and it may therefore be called a characteristic of the group. As a professional person, the captain distinctly combines economic and political life, earning his livelihood thereby, and acquiring the ethics and traits of his profession.

The conclusions reached so far are not presented dogmatically. Perhaps with a more refined and penetrating technique, the findings would be different. Be that as it may; no more is claimed for the conclusions than the technique permits. More comprehensive analysis lies with the psychologist, the psychoanalyst, and the statistician, or with some as yet unrecognized type of social analyst. A newer method is the social process or functional approach.

Though there is no typical precinct captain, there are similarities in the activities performed by these officials, to which we now turn.

4. THE LOCAL CLUB AND THE CANVASS

THE PRECINCT CAPTAIN'S VERSATILITY IS AMAZING. His activities range from routine political drudgery to less savory services such as shielding thieves from justice and distributing privileges in exchange for votes.

In addition to mass meetings—usually characterized by the presence of prominent candidates, troubadours, vaudeville, and martial music—party workers often use the more local group method, the club. The ward club plays a more important role than the precinct club, partly because of the election of aldermen and ward committeemen. Even so, it is usually only temporary, lasting merely throughout the local campaign.

Public job-holders, whose power and destiny are intimately related to those of the ward leader, are the nuclei of the ward club. These office-holders include the precinct captains, the judges of the Municipal Court, other elected officials residing in the locality, and all non-elected job-holders for the most part exempt from civil service standards and safeguards. The club is financed by this coterie. In one ward, a captain earning $6,000 a year as assistant state's attorney was asked to contribute $15 a month to his ward organization. Others made contributions according to their earnings and their agreements with the ward committeeman. One judge not only made a generous allowance to his ward club, but also assisted those captains within the ward who were in straitened circumstances. The responsibility of the ward club rested with the ward committeeman.

The ward club became the meeting place for all active workers. At various times, the voters in the district were permitted to use it for social purposes. Mrs. F, committeeman of a West Side ward, said: "The hall is let free of charge for weddings to any of the families living in the ward," and showed a list of social organizations which were scheduled to use it. Not all ward clubs had headquarters which they could share with the people in the locality. Some of the headquarters were a large room above a bank, the real estate office of an alderman, a poolroom, or the home of the ward committeeman. They were frequently bare rooms with many chairs rented for the campaign.

The theme of conversation in these ward headquarters was, naturally, "jobs." There was an air of camaraderie; people greeted each other by their Christian names. There was much swapping of political gossip, and, before an election, a great deal of combative enthusiasm for the approaching battle. Here, in addition to the general instructions given out by the ward committeeman to his workers at the mass-meetings special orders were issued individually to each precinct captain.

The precinct club, which is of immediate interest, was found less frequently than the ward club. Only one-fourth of the precinct captains maintained political clubs in their areas. These were usually organizations of workers, or of citizens interested in party affairs. The purpose of the club, in all sections of the city in which it was found, was to keep a few active persons together in order to have ready a working unit for an election. The club added continuity and sociability, but more than that, it served as a vote-holding unit.

The precinct clubs were financed by the captains and public office-holders of the neighborhood. Few were permanent fixtures —most of them existed only during campaigns, often simply through the whim of the local party representative. The meeting-place might be at the precinct captain's home, at the ward headquarters, at a neighborhood confectionery, in a pool-room, or in a so-called "soft-drink" parlor.

These clubs prevailed in the poorer areas; they were subsidiary to the ward organization. Gang feeling and loyalty to a particular person helped to sustain them. Sometimes the introduction of athletics bound the members to them more closely. Often, too, misdemeanors committed by boys brought them into these clubs. The staunchest workers in one club were a group of boys who had been arrested one night for rough-housing. The precinct captain, aided by the alderman, got them released. Out of gratitude they joined the club and some became his heelers.

A number of the captains organized district clubs including four or five precincts. They also encouraged the formation of a "Ladies Club," because "the wife controls the husband's vote." The men, however, were more frequently organized than the women. Even the children were not forgotten. The Barber Colts' Club was an organization of boys interested in baseball and politics and encouraged by the captain. Another baseball club was sponsored by a captain who was an ardent baseball fan. Every Sunday morning, he joined the boys of the neighborhood at their game. Through his friendship with the boys, he learned to know their parents and the eligible voters in their families. He endeared himself to his young playfellows by securing a part allotment in the district from the city administration. In return, captains frequently used children's groups to distribute buttons, flags, and other regalia during campaigns.

Social contacts are an extremely valuable adjunct to vote-getting. Affability and opportunities to display a pleasing personality to his constituents are of great importance to the precinct captain. Nor are party officials slow to recognize the importance of social connections. One captain joined a nonpartisan, social "good fellowship" club, and thus gained a wide acquaintance and many votes. Another belonged to the Master Plumbers' Association, the Catholic Order of Foresters, the Polish National

Alliance, the Polish Alma Mater, the Pan Club, the Midwest Sanitary Club, and the Avondale Improvement Club. One captain was chairman of eight clubs; he was an active church member, and a stockholder in a cooperative society. These clubs covered areas larger than the precinct, but nevertheless influenced the captain's power in his locality. The ward and precinct clubs were the usual settings for these contacts, since they gave the party agent the opportunity to meet his neighbors. Where there were no local clubs, the homes of captains were used.

About a third of the precinct officials arranged social activities for their neighborhoods. More captains in the Thompson faction and in the Democratic Party conducted these functions than in the Deneen faction. The social functions included smokers and stags for the men (4 per cent); more frequently, card parties, and in the middle-class and poor localities, "bunco," especially for women (more than 13 per cent); mixed socials, including dances, picnics, and ice cream parties (nearly 14 per cent); dances alone (4 per cent); picnics (2 per cent): The Kaffee Klatsch was also mentioned. Baseball clubs were on the agenda, with an eye for the first votes. One captain, a former saloon-keeper, regretted the disappearance of the saloon, for it had served as an excellent social center. A drink invariably brought a vote. After the Volstead Act, more politicians used the church to make their social contacts. Captains who did not take the Eighteenth Amendment very seriously arranged "gin and beer parties." At times, the larger party organizations, the district or ward clubs, planned these social activities, or distributed tickets to Riverview, an amusement park, or to special benefit movies.

When a mass meeting was called, the captains in the poor precincts invited the voters and conveyed them to the meeting hall, either in automobiles provided by the ward boss or by the ward organization. In the summer, the ward executives arranged picnics to which the precinct captains brought their constituents. Speeches and band music were the usual features of these occasions. Although social functions were used by the captains of all parties, they were arranged less often in first class residential areas.

In addition to such social techniques of vote-getting the party functionary utilized the canvass to solicit votes. A list of the voters was maintained by a general registration every four years, and by intermediate registrations before every primary and election. This registration system was decentralized and bi-partisan, conducted within the precinct by 5 paid officials, 3 judges and 2 clerks. These were supposed to be appointed by the Board of Election Commissioners, which is also bi-partisan, but were actually named by the precinct captain in the locality.

The precinct captain, interested in cultivating a reliable constituency, gave much care to developing a generous registry. After the registry was created, the captain proceeded to canvass the lists in his bailiwick to establish friendly relations with the voters.

In the intense factional campaign of 1928, and prior to the permanent registration law of 1936, only 75 per cent of the eligible voters registered. Both the "machine-workers" and the newspapers were excessively active. Their activity failed, however, to move many voters, whose apathy remained unassailable.

After registration, the election clerks required to canvass the registry to verify the registered lists. Since the clerks were chosen by their precinct captains, they wittingly or unwittingly served them by making a careless, superficial investigation of the questionable names on the registry, by ignoring discrepancies which should have disqualified the voters, or by committing other irregularities which helped their faction.

THE LOCAL CLUB AND THE CANVASS

The unit agents interviewed stated that they or their assistants canvassed the precincts, both before and after registration preceding the primary, and after the primary. This procedure was followed by the most active captains, usually in order to ascertain the preferences of the voter and to persuade him to vote the ticket. An early canvass gave the trained captain an index to the voters' preferences. Even though he might not be able to convert skeptics, he got a knowledge of the weak spots which needed special attention. This information was used to advantage when the ward committeeman collected the pledge cards which were signed during the canvass. This was of special importance in localities where money was distributed to influence voting.

The canvass is not a new nor a uniquely American method. Party secretaries or agents in other countries are acquainted with it. The successful canvasser, whether paid by a party machine or moved by his own political enthusiasm, chats easily, takes a warm interest in the family he is visiting, and, above all, has learned the art of being on the same plane with every one he meets.

Three quarters of the precinct emissaries canvassed their localities; a much smaller number used both the precinct club and the canvass. These methods were used least often in the first-class residential areas. The technique of the canvass was determined largely by the localities in which it was used. In the better middle-class and the first-class residential areas, the canvasser rarely got beyond the front door; the only way the voter could be reached was through a social club or on the golf course. Frequently the captain engaged quarters in a large apartment hotel, learned to know his neighbors, and then approached them; sometimes he picked his lieutenants from among the residents of these hotels, and thus gained adherents.

In the poorer localities, the precinct captain resorted to subterfuge. He brought inexpensive gifts to the children or distributed calendars; he catered to the interests of the household by commenting on the excellent qualities of Cardinal Mundelein to a Catholic, or on the learned and benevolent attributes of Rabbi Wise to a Jew. He was always ready with his services. Surely the householder had a small errand for him, a tax bill to be paid, a fishing permit to be secured. Perhaps a voter wanted tickets to a prize fight, or to one of the amusement parks. A burned-out fuse turned the canvasser into an amateur electrician —one such situation brought a lucky precinct captain 10 votes. The offer of a job to the head of a large household of eligible voters was another canvasser's method. When proffered generosities failed, the canvasser tried to engage the franchise-holder to work for him on election day as a subterfuge for outright buying of his vote, which is illegal. If all his blandishments failed, he took defeat philosophically, making a genial exit.

In lodging-house areas, the strategy of the canvasser was different. Votes were bargained for in blocks through the owners of the "hobo" hotels. One diligent precinct captain tried to canvass each roomer in a "flop house," but found the procedure too expensive. The precinct captain sometimes owned a lodging-house, and by allowing free lodging for short periods of time or special concessions in rent, he gained votes without canvassing. Sometimes the clerks in these rooming-houses were hired as canvassers; they combined electioneering with their other duties.

The more ambitious local mediaries, especially in the poor and middle-class areas, did their own canvassing. "I do it twelve months a year, and I keep tab of the people as they move in and out of the precinct," was stated by a number of these captains. Some canvassed their areas twice a year, others only during important campaigns, and still others visited their constituents before and after registration. A great many of the officials insisted that without a canvass, they accomplished nothing, and that they "pounded doors" four times a year at least. Some of the officials arranged to be the last political agent to visit the family, because it gave them every chance to refute their opponent's arguments. In the better residential areas, or in areas so dilapidated that the precinct captain no longer lived in them, lieutenants were paid to canvass. In some such areas the precinct captains made one canvass to determine the tone of the constituency, but sent lieutenants to persuade the unconvinced voters. Sometimes the wives of the captains canvassed the districts.

The appeals used during the canvass varied. The "bread-and-butter" argument was most convincing in the poorer areas. The canvasser stated that he was holding a governmental job which depended upon the number of votes he could muster on primary or election day. In such localities a vote was considered far less important than a job.

The party managers, ward chiefs, or a regional campaign committee chosen for this purpose formulated the campaign slogans. These were passed along to the captains to be popularized by them. During the 1928 primary, "prosperity" and "America First," were used by the Thompsonites, and "decency and clean government" by the Deneenites. The Democratic captains supported one or the other of the Republican factions on primary day, but on election day, they backed their own party.

One factotum stated that politics was like salesmanship; the more highly advertised the commodity, the surer the sale; the talking-point counted most. A number of captains distributed pictures of their candidates when they canvassed. In the localities where pledge cards were signed, the psychological effect was to bind the voter. In a number of the West Side wards, the ward committeemen insisted on pledge cards because they gauged the activities of the captains. Canvassers frequently visited their constituents alone; sometimes they went as a committee, finding conversation more readily stimulated and the element of fear reduced.

The ward committeeman generally decided how frequently canvasses should be made; this depended on the type of campaign and on the mobility of the citizens in the area. It was the business of the captain to know the voters he was responsible for. Some captains kept card catalogs; they procured the names of the voters from the public registry, and corrected their cards as the voters moved in and out of the precinct. The consensus among the captains was that an effectively executed canvass was the best direct technique to win votes.

Other propaganda methods used by captains included sending letters, pamphlets, or pictures of candidates; arranging rallies and meetings (usually in conjunction with the ward organization), and encouraging the voters to read the newspapers which were favorable to their cause.

But the club, the social activities of the precinct captain, and the canvass are not sufficient to hold a political machine together; other techniques are necessary as well. These will be discussed in the following chapters.

5. MORE BREAD THAN CIRCUSES

Assistance to people in want or in trouble is another political strategy. State and private aid often fail to reach all who need help, nor has organized society a monopoly on altruistic impulse; it cannot bind the "urge to help" into institutions, nor can it compel all who are in need to knock only at its doors. Kindness of the poor to each other is universal. There is an unfailing response by the poor to the distresses of their less fortunate neighbors, even when to give may mean distress.

> The kindness which a poor man shows his neighbor is doubtless heightened by the consciousness that he may be in distress himself next week; he therefore stands by his friend when he gets too drunk to care for himself, when he loses his wife or child, when he is evicted for the non-payment of rent, or when he is arrested for a petty crime.*

In a locality where political standards are undeveloped and plastic, the poor expect similar favors from their political representatives. The captain living in the poorer neighborhood tends to adhere to the moral code set by his neighbors, but he has greater power than they because of his position. He functions to satisfy the social needs of his constituency and in so doing binds his neighbors to return past favors. He may be thoroughly sincere in his deeds of kindness; he may honestly enjoy the pleasure of being spoken of as a "good fellow" and humanely desire to alleviate suffering. These most laudable impulses may gradu-

* Jane Addams, *Democracy and Social Ethics* (New York, 1902).

ally change under pressure of the need for votes into the desire to put his people under obligation.

On the other hand, the person who receives aid gives with his voting support a commodity prized highly by the local party agent. He is not a beggar asking for bread, but an independent human being with a marketable vote. As far as the community is concerned, the demoralizing aspect enters when kindly impulses are made a cloak for the satisfaction of personal ambitions.

The extent of the basic benevolence of the party official in a large metropolis was gauged by the 600 captains interviewed in Chicago; the reports from other large municipalities substantiated the findings. The Assembly district leader of New York renders the same service; it is generally known that the success of Tammany Hall is based on its charitable deeds to the poor. Data regarding the Philadelphia Republican precinct committeemen are comparable.

The testimony of the captains was not verified, as the names and addresses of the recipients of their kindness were not obtainable. Except when a constituent betrayed the local boss, it was presumably the latter's policy not to disclose the names of those who had been the objects of his beneficence.

Again we must begin with the charitable deeds of the ward committeeman for there was a definite cleavage between his acts and those of the captain. Often the ward organization appropriated a definite sum to be spent for charity. The 41st Ward (Thompson Faction) spent $1,000 on charity in one year. The 24th Ward (Democrats) spent $1,500 a year for coal alone. The precinct captain recommended those who were to be helped. The alderman might also refer deserving cases. Sometimes the "lady members" of the political party, representing a larger area, assumed responsibility for the party's charities. The captain was in all instances the channel through which the wants of his constituents were satisfied. It was he who called upon the ward committeeman, the alderman, or even the county agent when he was not himself to furnish the necessary service. If a voter applied directly to any of the higher officials, he was referred to his local party agent, or information about him was procured from the captain, whose recommendation was usually followed. There were times when the captain individually raised funds to meet the needs of his district; at other times, he was too poor or too insignificant to have any personal power.

The field study showed that more than 49 per cent of the precinct functionaries in all Chicago areas furnished food, 42.2 per cent supplied coal, and 38.4 per cent provided rent. As might be expected, the captains living in first-class residential areas rendered no such service; most of it was found in the poor residential localities. The captain in one such locality paid the rent of a voter for the seven months of his unemployment. In another instance, the ward boss was the largest property owner in the area. Whenever any of the constituents of his faction in the region became delinquent in the payment of rent, the captain arranged with his superior not to press for payment, especially when he was certain of the tenant's vote. In eviction cases the captain interceded for the tenant by making a part-payment on the rent due and thus reinstating the tenant. The landlord might be satisfied by a special favor at City Hall in lieu of rent. Sometimes when dispossess cases were brought to court, the captain acted as the intermediary between the dispossessed tenant and the government. Clothing was frequently distributed to voters living in the poorer areas. Truant children, who stayed home because they had no clothes, were the special concern of one very diligent captain.

Precinct captains manifested further interest in children by helping widowed mothers to secure pensions, by arranging for the adoption of children, by procuring birth certificates or work certificates, or if the situation demanded it, by preventing the under-age child from procuring an employment permit, or by obtaining the transfer of a child from one school to another. In one striking instance, the captain succeeded in maintaining a child at school although the school psychologist had declared the child subnormal and had recommended his removal. At another time a disobedient pupil was reinstated after dismissal from school.

The foreign-born parent and the American child frequently clash in their views, and the captain steps in as family adjuster. In one family the parents objected to the numerous callers their daughter received at home; they were advised by the party worker that their attitude was harmful to the daughter. Much to the distress of another parent, the daughter had formed the habit of staying out late evenings. The party captain convinced the girl that such pranks were foolish, and persuaded her to mend her ways.

Some precinct dignitaries adjusted juvenile misdemeanors and thefts. The kindness showered upon the child frequently served to gain the confidence of the adults in the family, and eventually their votes. Forty per cent of the precinct captains in all the areas served as juvenile guidance advisors, the largest proportion being in poor residential areas.

The precinct captains functioned also in the adjustment of domestic difficulties; 30.2 per cent rendered this service. In one instance the captain was asked to prevent an Italian from beating his wife. Another captain helped a mother of ten children get a divorce from a drunkard, and a third intervened in the domestic affairs of a policeman who shot his wife; a temporary reconciliation was effected. In still another instance, a widow who had remarried, but who was unhappy because she had found her second husband inferior to the first, was advised that second marriages were usually made for convenience. A captain secured the release of a workingman, father of two children from Bridewell, where he had been sent because, crazed by "moonshine," he had attempted to slash his wife's throat. One party worker said that in domestic upheavals he tried to reconcile the husband and wife, but if this were futile, he encouraged and helped them to secure a divorce.

In illness and bereavement, warm sympathy made lasting attachments between families and their local captain. "To visit the sick, and bury the dead," was an established political practice. Nearly 60 per cent provided some form of aid to those needing medical care. Most frequently this help was furnished through public agencies. A physician in a public institution who owed his appointment to politics was expected to arrange hospitalization for the constituents of his benefactors. Some of the precinct captains sent private doctors to the sick; some reported them to public institutions. If a patient was already in a hospital and was dissatisfied with the care he was receiving, his transfer to another hospital was arranged. Many of the precinct captains or their wives visited the sick, brought flowers, conveyed them to or from the hospital, and otherwise ministered to their needs.

In case of death, the efficient captain, throughout the poorer localities, was usually present to add his sympathy and to offer comfort. No conscientious captain ever missed a funeral. More than 54 per cent of the captains reported they had attended funerals. Sometimes relatives requested "decent" burial for a poor relative. One Negro applied for a "right" burial for his son; and the captain not only saved the man from potter's field but also paid all funeral expenses. Flowers were customarily sent to funerals; one captain complained that he still owed for flowers he had sent to the last funeral he attended. Political workers often acted as pallbearers, or provided transportation for relatives and friends of the deceased, sometimes having their wives serve as chauffeurs. A precinct captain aided two Polish widows to arrange for the burial of their husbands, killed in accidents; the county was made to pay all the expenses.

Even as the precinct factotum mourned with his neighbors, so he rejoiced with them. More than 25 per cent attended weddings, a number much smaller, however, than those who attended funerals. A few party agents even attended christenings.

During the Christmas season, more than 70 per cent of the captains sent greetings or more substantial presents. Twenty-three baskets were given by one captain. In one instance, the captain sent a basket to a recent divorcee in his locality; in another a kind-hearted Irish captain carried one of the two turkeys his wife had prepared for his family to a needy widow in the district. Usually the ward organization provided the baskets distributed by the captains. Four thousand baskets were sent in one ward. Frequently dances were arranged to raise money for financing such efforts. An unscrupulous citizen sometimes managed to get baskets from more than one captain.

Another function of the captains of all parties was to provide the needy with employment. The officials found work for their constituents in local governmental offices, in semi-public concerns, and with private firms. Nearly 55 per cent supplied their constituents with government jobs; nearly 33 per cent in the city government, 21 per cent in unspecified government offices 5 per cent in the county, about 2 per cent in the Sanitary District, more than 1 per cent in the federal offices, nearly 2 per cent with the park boards, less than 1 per cent with the courts. These were either permanent jobs or temporary, lasting from 60 to 90 days, distributed usually before a primary or an election; some were merely payroll jobs with no service requirement. Such jobs were distributed by the captains in all three classes of residential areas, but fewest government jobs were provided in the most prosperous areas.

Twelve government jobs were obtained by one captain; others secured 7 or 8 jobs. A small number provided positions for policemen, firemen, janitors, teachers, and school clerks. The position of life guard on a public beach was supplied by one captain.

The captain's job quota depended on the patronage of his ward committeeman. More of the Thompson captains found employment for the constituents in the city administration than in the other governments; more of the Democrats found jobs for their friends in the county; more of the Deneen captains placed their adherents in federal offices. The patronage in the Sanitary District and the park boards was divided.

Local officers provided their friends with a wide range of non-government jobs; nearly 70 per cent had helped their constituents find such employment. Through the public utilities, the captains often found work for their adherents. When the captain lacked influence, the ward committeeman or the party secretary acted as employment agent. Among the private concerns to which the precinct captains sent their adherents were the taxicab companies; Sears, Roebuck and Company; the stockyards; and the numerous construction companies. If a captain owned a business, unemployed voters were often sent to him.

In the poorer areas, where the demand for jobs was greatest, the ward headquarters served as an employment bureau. The jobs supplied were usually clerical work and unskilled labor. The captains' political power, especially in the poor and middle-class localities, depended in part on the number of jobs at their disposal.

Sixty-four per cent of the precinct captains provided their

constituents with legal aid, the larger part of such service being in the poor residential areas. Most frequently the captains acted as intermediaries, and directed their clients to lawyers.

In some localities, the mediary served also as a community agent who intervened to remedy unsatisfactory conditions. He exerted pressure on the various administrative agencies of the city to collect the garbage, to lighten dark streets and alleys, to mend torn-up pavements, to clean blocked sewers, and to provide adequate police protection. One captain succeeded, after much effort, in having an officer stationed at a dangerous crossing.

Sometimes the captain intervened between his neighbors, or between the individual and the community. One cautioned against throwing mattresses into an alley. One prevented the owner of a pie factory from throwing refuse into the streets. One intervened between two women who threw ashes in front of each other's door-step when they quarrelled. One restrained an apartment builder from disobeying the building laws, and secured the withdrawal of the building permit when the frontage of the proposed building was not according to city regulation. This captain's property would have suffered in value if he had not.

More than 63 per cent had taken an interest in maintaining their districts in reasonably good order. Only 32 per cent of those who lived in first-class residential areas performed such services.

A multitude of miscellaneous beneficences placed the precinct captain in the category of the voters' friend. He lent money and tools; he supplied a young man with cash enough to marry, he acted as matchmaker; he ran errands; he provided tickets for places of entertainment—these usually cost him nothing. A woman captain ironed clothes and cared for a neighbor's baby. Others helped to build a garage, got dogs out of the pound, and even advised when the pipes froze. In short, the precinct captain granted any favor which strengthened his political position. The captains of all factions and parties gave about the same amount of such "fix-it" services, mostly in the poorer districts.

The relationship between social service agencies and precinct captains has long been a subject of surmise. Judging by the captains questioned, nearly 50 per cent had had some such contact. The public social service agency was used more frequently than the private agency. In one instance, a woman precinct official, employed as a social worker in a public agency, took care of the needy for her party colleagues. Applicants frequently were sent to the Cook County Bureau of Public Welfare. The local party official preferred to aid his constituents or to use the assistance of the ward committeeman or alderman.

Party agents were critical of private social service agencies claiming that such agencies used most of their funds for those on the "inside," and not for the welfare of the poor. The "red tape" and the long-drawn-out investigations were also criticized. The private agencies were also accused of being too technical; they "studied" the poor too much. An Italian captain objected to them because the applicants had to beg for the things they needed.

Inquiry made of persons in charge of the private and public agencies in the city, including the settlements, showed that the captains would frequently use these agencies to further their own ends. Records in the branch offices of the United Charities showed that captains sometimes intervened for their constituents, accompanying them to the office or sending letters to explain the need for help. Frequently they camouflaged themselves as the applicant's friend. Social workers in the poor localities testified to instances in which the captains found employment for some of their clients. The assistant supervisor of the United Charities of Chicago was emphatic in the belief that the family case agencies were being exploited by party workers and that the latter often took credit for many services rendered by social workers.

The executives of the public social service agencies stated that they knew that captains referred cases to their assistants, but they could not estimate the extent to which the practice was carried. Said one official:

> Because of the precinct captain's interest in the difficulties of his community, and because of his knowledge of the sources of public relief, he is inevitably the means through which a great many needy individuals are brought in contact with the public relief agencies.*

The receiving supervisor of the Cook County Hospital stated that the captains usually secured admission for their constituents through the alderman, the county commissioners, or someone higher in the party hierarchy. The head residents of social settlements said that captains had referred people to them, but that no records were available.

Many of the workers in the public agencies were themselves captains. The assistant superintendent of the Cook County Bureau of Public Welfare had formerly been a captain and was at the time of the interview a ward committeeman in the Democratic Party.

An outstanding difference between the relief technique of the precinct captain and that of the trained social worker was that the former did not "clear" a case to learn whether the applicant was receiving aid from other sources. He never investigated the person who sought help. His main interest was to do favors, to be constantly at the beck and call of his constituents. If they required aid, he wished to be present to provide it. No request was too insignificant for him; he bought ice cream for the chil-

* JOSEPH L. MOSS, Cook County Bureau of Public Welfare.

dren, and mended their kites. He pointedly assumed the role of the Good Samaritan, with none of the "grilling" and "nagging" attributed to social workers.

In the light of the experience of organized social work, the benevolences of the precinct captain did not appear constructive. They were not systematically managed or recorded. The precinct captain wished merely to please and satisfy in order to enhance his political power. His services were immediate and palliative. The result was frequently that his help was futile.

The services performed by the precinct functionary so resembled those of the social worker that a question arises whether the former might not entirely replace the latter. Certainly the captain had this much in his favor; he knew the people in his locality individually. It was to his advantage to serve his constituents well. He had entree to the governmental agencies; in many instances he genuinely delighted in occupying himself with the worries of his "friends" and in serving as their eager lackey. Moreover, in those areas where social work was most necessary, he was frequently regarded with respect, because he was usually superior to the residents in education and economic status.

Another official whose activities overlap those of the precinct captain is the policeman. A manual for policemen reads, "When a person is found destitute or requires medical attention, investigate the case fully. If he needs the attention of a doctor, summon an ambulance. If he requires the necessities of life and is unable to walk to the commissioner of charities, get him there. . . . Any reasonable request of a sick or injured person should be complied with by the patrolman."* The patrolman comes in direct contact with the offender and often knows the less formal aspects of his life. He often helps the needy, but more

* Captain Cornelius Cahalane, *A Course of Study for Policemen Everywhere*, p. 867.

frequently he directs them to the appropriate public agency.

From the viewpoint of organized society, the activities of the social worker may be classified as positive beneficence; they are conscious efforts to adapt individuals to society. The outgoing friendliness of the precinct mediary cannot, however, be considered a negative quality. Surely there are times in the lives of those with limited opportunities, living in squalor and need, when a friendly smile or the respect of an equal may be more valuable than a loaf of bread. The standardized kindness of a young social worker may sometimes lack human qualities and may fail to furnish the sympathy and heartfelt understanding which is so essential. The motives or ideals of the precinct captain may be questionable, but the technique he has developed for treating the people in his locality, his geniality, kindness, and sympathy are noteworthy.

Contrasting the three agents, we find that the patrolman does not usually live in the beat he patrols; in fact, his beat is frequently shifted. The social worker does not live in the district to which she is assigned; the settlement-worker does, but her standard of living is usually so different from that of her neighbors that she has no direct contact with them. The captain makes his home in the locality which he serves. From a sociological viewpoint, his relations with his constituents are conducted on a primary level; the social worker's interactions are on a secondary level or are entirely formal. The success of the precinct captain, especially in areas peopled by newly made citizens, depends, in fact, on just such informal interactions; they are the only kind his constituents understand and trust. As long as the present industrial, social, and political regime continues in the urban community, in essentially its present form, there is little likelihood that these three types of social agents will move in the same orbit or that any one of them will replace the other.

6. FIXING: A FRIEND AT COURT

THE PRECINCT CAPTAIN'S GENEROSITY IS NOT LIMITED TO financial favors. His position depends also on his connection with the government, and on his ability to intercede for the individual in the application of the law. This is especially true in the districts where newly naturalized Americans make their homes, although the same condition is found in "hundred per cent" American localities.

Is it any wonder that many foreigners in the larger municipalities, unaccustomed to American institutions, look upon the politician, who shakes hands warmly and speaks English as their friend and the interpreter of American life? It is not surprising that when he gets in trouble with the government, the newcomer seeks the help and advice of the man who is ready to give this help. It would be surprising if the meagerly educated American did not lean on his political representative when he is in need or in trouble. Men living near the masses of the people recognize the value of the simple and more primitive human interests and ways. They realize that the people clamor for the informal, for the warm human qualities of social interrelationship. the people misinterpret the harsher, more formal governmental and private agencies.

Chicago, like every great American city, has an elaborate organization concerned with humanizing the law. This organization thrives within the government, and constitutes the non-bureaucratic manipulator of governmental institutions. Favors, graft, and protection are its mainstay. Its chief resources include the manipulation of the taxing machinery, the placement of public funds with anticipation of splitting the profits, the letting of contracts, the protection and defense of bootleggers and of various other types of criminals. Tax fixing and adjusting, sundry payments for enactment and blocking of legislation, control of the election machinery, perquisites and miscellaneous adjustments—all are important cogs in this machine.

The existence of this organization on a large scale was unmistakably exposed in the 1928 primary. The newspapers described in detail the combination of influences and agencies concerned with controlling the political situation by furnishing immunity from the law. Its hierarchy of givers and getters, bound in an intricate network of privilege and favors at the top of the ladder, was after the year's election, temporarily toppled from its lofty position.

But what of the little men, those who represent the political organization in the smallest districts? The local functionary's greatest concern is to cultivate a constituency which will go his way. When he finds that purely social activities or benevolent acts or organization techniques fail, he seeks other means. He casts about for a group which he may bind to him, for whom he may do favors, and from whom he may seeks favors in return. The wants of the very rich and of the poor may be different in form, but for both he seeks to be a friend at court and in the tax office. The local dignitary has learned from practical experience the advantage he may reap by doing favors, especially when they concern concessions from the government. They give him added power and prestige; public office is held in great esteem by the foreign voters who come from countries where government officials are more autocratic.

The more glaringly inefficient governmental agencies are the most subject to pressure from party officials. The legislative, judicial, and administrative branches are all subjected on occasion to intervention by political bosses. In Chicago, the political parties had patronage jobs in the administrative bureaus of the city, in the Board of Assessors, and in the Board of Review (then still in existence); in the Sanitary District, the Municipal and County Courts, and the federal agencies.

The taxing agencies were found to be subjected most frequently to the precinct captain's fixing procedures. Seventy per cent of the precinct officials said they had adjusted taxes. The main taxes in Illinois were the general property tax, the annual franchise taxes on corporations, the insurance company taxes, the inheritance taxes, the motor vehicle license taxes, and a number of miscellaneous license taxes and fees. In Cook County, including Chicago, the Board of Assessors, composed of five members, elected for terms of six years, assessed real estate and personal property, and had general supervision over assessments. The Board of Review, composed of three members elected for six years, reviewed and equalized the assessments made by the Board of Assessors. The members of the Board of Review received salaries of $10,000 a year, and members of the Board of Assessors, $9,000, making a total expenditure of $75,000 a year. A statute of 1898 provided for a quadrennial reassessment of real estate.

The forms of taxation involved in the study of the precinct captains were real estate and personal property taxes. Under the law, all property, both real and personal, must be assessed at its full cash value. Although fairly equitable methods of evaluating real property have been devised, it has been far more difficult to find a way of ascertaining the value of personal property. There are, however, forms of property that are "personal," in a social as well as in an economic sense, such as clothing, furniture, and so on. There is also the intangible property. These forms of property are exceedingly difficult to evaluate and their assessment leads to guess work and manipulation. The individual citizen is frequently unwilling to disclose to a taxing board the full value of his personal property. When the taxpayer feels, rightly or wrongly, that the amount assessed against his personal or real property is exorbitant, he frequently calls upon the precinct captain to reduce his bill. The party agent serves him readily. The success of the precinct captain in fixing bills depends upon the power of his party on the taxing boards.

As a result of these tax-adjusting activities carried on by the precinct captains and other party workers, Chicago finds itself with a battery of extra-legal "boards of revision," maintained by the political organizations. Since these "boards" were built to a great extent to "correct" some of the imperfections of the tax system, they are vitally concerned with its continuance, thus completing a vicious circle.

The economic background for this political control lies in the apparent apathy of the legitimate business and financial interests, in the over-stimulated professional zeal of the members of the Board of Review and of the assessors, in the innumerable officials connected with the taxing system who derive a direct livelihood through it, and in the beneficiary groups which are favored by the taxing bodies. The total of taxes remitted to favored groups was said to amount to some $30,000,000 annually.

The fear of retaliation by assessing officials is another very influential economic element. Thousands of property holders have been held in a constant state of apprehension as to their assessments from year to year. This fear compelled many of them to make political contributions, to maintain silence and to prevent them from serving on committees devoted to correcting the defects of the system.

The weakness of the taxing system was most obvious in the precinct, and the precinct captain took full advantage of this. Personal and real property taxes were most frequently adjusted. Sixty-five per cent of the captains stated that they also adjusted assessments of intangible property. One captain said he had saved for his constituents from $15 to $100 a year. Tax fixing was not limited to one faction or party or to a particular residential area.

The local functionary's procedure in tax fixing varied. In some instances, he contacted the taxing agencies personally, in others he sought the aid of the ward committeeman, the alderman, or some acquaintance serving on the Board of Assessors or the Board of Review. Some captains merely aided their uneducated neighbors to make out tax schedules, or directed their complaining constituents to the office of the board for a reconsideration of the assessments. Constituents with small bills might be encouraged not to pay their personal property taxes, because amounts below $25 were not pressed. Frequently property owners were merely given "advice" which would enable them to avoid the full force of the law. A few captains actually made the rounds of their localities to collect tax schedules which needed fixing, and took them to the Board of Review for modification. A number of party agents took a hand only when they felt that taxes were unjust. In one instance, a widowed mother living in one of the poorer precincts was taxed $29.50 for furniture which was old and worn. The captain in that area called on a friend in the state's attorney's office, who knew someone on the Board of Review, and the entire assessment was dropped. Usually no charges were made by the local officers when they adjusted taxes; they merely sought to put the voter under obligation. Sometimes, however, they did charge, even as much as 50 per cent of the reduction.

Political intervention of captains was also found to affect city government and finance in a variety of ways. The trail of the captain led to many city agencies, such as building, health, police, fire, weights and measures, and such activities as the enforcement of ordinances or franchises, and the issuance or withdrawal of licenses and permits. Forty-four per cent of the captains said that they had secured permits of every variety for their adherents: peddlers', milk, garage, and basket permits; building permits led the list, but there were many others.*

One mediary helped his neighbor set aside an order by the Fire Department to change the location of a stairway at considerable expense and inconvenience. He accomplished this feat through friends he had in the Fire Department who desired promotion. These ambitious city employees were induced not to make an issue of forgetting even to send notices, and in the end, nothing was done. In another case, the captain made it possible for the building contractor to place a window on the side of a house forbidden by the city's zoning ordinance. In some of the city wards, the captains specialized in the fixing of specific complaints. On occasions when the local "fixer" paid for the privileges he secured for his constituents, the amount was very small, not over $2. More often the licenses or permits were procured without any remuneration to the city, just by "pull." The extent of the precinct agent's intervention in the License Department of the city, as well as in the many other departments, can only be guessed; no accurate records are available. This form of assistance, moreover, was not restricted to the captains of any one party nor to those living in a particular area of the city. Whenever the captain lacked friends in the area where pressure was needed, he

---

* For a blind man to sell pencils in the "Loop"; for a constituent to use certain electric signs and fixtures; for a voter to sell Christmas trees; for a citizen to tear down a building; for a colored man to operate a cart; for a property owner to build a garage within an alley in the violation of a fire ordinance; for a hospital superintendent to maintain quiet in a hospital zone; for a declarant to peddle; a hunting and fishing license for a constituent; for a wealthy constituent to build a forty-two apartment building by procuring an amendment of the zoning law for the district; dancing space in a park for a dance hall proprietor.

called upon influential members'of the party hierarchy for assistance.

The judicial system, especially the machinery of criminal justice, is also subject to "fixing" by political agents. A study of criminal justice administration shows a lack of permanence of tenure precluding any continuity of policy. It also shows the administration to be impeded by a heavy burden of politics, which frequently interferes with its workings when persons of political consequence or their friends are concerned.

The judicial machinery of Cook County and Chicago is on the whole notoriously inefficient and wasteful. There are 6 categories of courts in Chicago: superior, circuit, county, probate, criminal, and municipal. The jurisdiction of all these courts is concurrent in many respects and yet cases arise in which not one of them has complete and comprehensive jurisdiction. There are 48 judges of the circuit and superior courts who are to a large extent free from centralized administrative control. The duplication in the courts is complicated by a duplication in clerical and other subsidiary judicial officers, such as sheriffs, who serve in courts of county-wide jurisdiction, and bailiffs, who serve the municipal court with a city-wide jurisdiction.

Direct responsibility for the enforcement of the criminal law generally is divided between the police and the office of prosecuting attorney. Though the prosecuting attorney is responsible for trying criminals, he is largely dependent upon the police for the detection of crime and the arrest of offenders, and for securing the evidence upon which successful prosecution rests. In the larger cities, and especially in Chicago, the municipal court has jurisdiction in criminal matters. Its jurisdiction, however, is actually limited to that held formerly by the justices of the peace. In all cases of felony it is limited to binding over for the grand jury. The prosecuting attorney has absolute power to nolle prosse; furthermore, he can ignore the municipal court by pro-curing indictments directly before the grand jury. In the circuit and superior courts, archaic methods of procedure obtain, with the result that conviction is secured in only a small fraction of the cases. Responsibility for enforcement of the criminal law is thus diffused instead of concentrated.

Another serious defect of the system is the practice of choosing judges by election, a practice which tends to throw the court into politics and militates against securing the most de-sirable type of judge. Like most elective offices, the judgeships, clerkships, and the office of sheriff are accompanied by many additional jobs which are distributed among party henchmen. In the office of the clerk of the municipal court alone, there are 350 available jobs, and the judges of the court have at their disposal 660 jobs involving an annual expenditure of more than $1,500,-000 in salaries. With the county judicial offices included, there about 1,000 jobs, involving an expenditure of over $2,000,000. These positions, filled as a rule not on a basis of fitness, but as political spoils, represent real power. The judges are frequently committed to the tactics of the politicians, more so because of the short judicial term.

One of the most difficult problems connected with prosecution has to do with bail, a matter particularly subject to "fixing." Nearly 40 per cent of the local party officers said they had fur-nished bail. The charges for which bail was given varied from drunkenness to grand larceny, including murder, gambling, and carrying concealed weapons.* Three to four calls a day from

* A few specific examples of cases for which bond was given are notated: larceny; disorderly conduct and larceny; man arrested as suspect, found in the company of a person with a bad record; boy held in the detention home for refusing to go to school; engaged in a confidence game; man held for colliding with an official in an automobile accident; gambling; drunkenness; knife fights; tampering with the mails; stealing; neighborhood fights; truck-men who killed a boy in the neighborhood; woman whose dog had been run-ning about the precinct unmuzzled; selling fire crackers on the Fourth of July; non-payment of alimony; boys arraigned for breaking windows.

the police station were not unusual for many of the local "fixers" in some of the poorer areas. A few kept cash on hand for such emergencies. The "fix" sometimes started with the police officers, the janitors of the court, the clerks or bailiffs. The trail might lead through the ward committeemen to the judge, in all cases depending upon the influence of the "fixer" and the power of his party; the judge and the bailiff usually belonged to the same party faction. For minor offenses in the local police station, some precinct captains found the promise of a few dollars to an official or the assurance of a job to an ordinary "cop" sufficient to do the trick. When more serious offenses were involved, the judge was reached through the bailiff, or by a party representative higher in the hierarchy, who had power to threaten the defeat of the judge in the next election if the "fix" did not go through.

A captain sometimes refused to furnish bail, sign bonds, or take any part in "fixing," for fear of censure from his constituents, or because he found the task too troublesome. In some localities the constituency made no such demands upon him. Nearly 40 per cent of the captains in all Chicago areas said they had furnished bond, given cash bail, or used their influence to secure release of persons arrested. Of these, more than 43 per cent lived in the poor residential areas, 38 per cent in the middle-class districts, and nearly 15 per cent in the first class areas. A comparison of the captains in their respective factions showed that less than 30 per cent of the Deneen captains had furnished this aid, contrasted with over 40 per cent of captains in the Thompson Republican faction and the Democratic Party.

Traffic violations also lent themselves readily to "fixing." According to the study, the offenses were usually parking or speeding. Most of the active stewards, irrespective of faction or party or of the particular locality in which they lived, were involved in this activity. More than half of the captains in the middle-class areas "fixed" tickets for their constituents; nearly half of those in good residential areas did the same; only 42 per cent in the poor areas served their friends in this capacity, mainly because fewer constituents had cars. The frequency of the practice among the captains of all areas, nearly 40 per cent, was well known to the local judiciary. It was notoriously easy to have a parking or speeding notice dropped. In one instance, the precinct captain saved a family $75 in fines and got ten votes. A former bailiff related that he was able to earn a handsome fee by submitting a list of names given him by professional adjusters to the judge, who, when in good humor, signed without reviewing the charges. Most of the precinct "fixings" were effected by the ward committeeman or the alderman after the cases were reported to them by the precinct captains.

A few of the precinct captains also acknowledged "fixing" of jury personnel by securing the release of persons summoned to serve. One captain explained that frequently a day in court was a heavy financial loss to his constituents and he undertook to provide substitutes. Jury "fixing" is also a part of the political machine's activity, but for obvious reasons this feat is usually accomplished through intermediaries and is rarely acknowledged by the party agents. The pressure of spoilsmen upon judges is a well-known practice in Chicago, where judges are frequently ward committeemen and dependent upon party support for election. The "fixing" of election cases with henchmen of the precinct captains indicted for vote frauds, was also found to exist.

The functionary also intervened for his constituency in the local federal agencies, especially in the Naturalization Bureau. The federal law regarding naturalization presents many confusing details to a foreigner, and the precinct "fixer" is very ready to help him out of the confusion. In fact, 68 per cent of the captains interviewed said they engaged in this type of activity. Party affiliation made no appreciable difference. In the good residential areas, fewer captains performed the function. In general the captains filled out naturalization blanks, acted as witnesses, taught the language and coached on the questionnaire, spoke to the clerk of the court or the naturalization examiner in behalf of the declarant, organized classes in civics, paid the required fees, and provided every conceivable suggestion and aid.*

A precinct captain who had assisted 62 aliens within 15 years declared that he felt it was this service particularly which impressed the voters in his locality. Whenever he helped a prospective citizen, he invoked his promise to vote for his party.

Frequently the applicant made personal demands upon the captain. In a West Side locality, such a declarant made all arrangements to bring his wife and child from Russia, but was advised to wait until he had secured his second papers. He appeared before the Naturalization Examiners who, for some technical reason, refused to pass him. The district court judge requested the man to return in six months. In desperation, he

---

* Twelve consecutive reports in the survey read: produced several naturalization blanks which he was filling out for some of his constituents; when asked if he filled most of these out before an election, he evaded by saying, "Oh, just any time"; his adherents are 8 per cent foreigners and "need guidance like children." He looks after them, and acts as witness whenever necessary; "She is constantly being called upon to help her constituents become naturalized citizens. She has organized classes in the essentials of citizenship for those in the precinct preparing for the examination"; "Mrs. D. has an organization in her ward which presents an American flag to each new citizen"; "Mr. M. has acted as witness three times, and he has coached eight applicants"; there are six lawyers in his precinct organization and the captain calls upon them for help; he has helped one barber and a shoemaker to secure their citizenship papers; in thirty-four years of political work, Mr. Z. has assisted one hundred and fifty foreigners become citizens; Mr. H. makes it his special concern to encourage the women in his bailiwick to secure their citizenship; Mrs. S. has acted as the ward agent for those seekng citizenship; Mr. P. has a case a day; Mr. R. is particularly concerned with the people in the precinct who have their first papers

sought help from his captain, who interceded, arranging for a re-examination within a week. The captain was a member of the political party which had federal patronage, and was well acquainted with the clerk of the court, who was a member of the same party.

In short, the activities of the captain reach all branches of local government, and his success is determined by the power of the party to which he belongs. Clearly enough, in a prosperous urban community like Chicago, administrative and judicial services are especially colored by the "spoils" system. Where the system is in full operation, the officials tend to use their office as a means of indirect graft or outright frud. Being part of a huge machine built upon this principle, an official, either elected or appointed by the machination of the party, can scarcely escape the demand that he regard his party allies as entitled to special consideration when he is in a position to grant favors. With weak laws and a rapid turnover of officials, the tendency becomes all the stronger and the power of resistance weaker.

From the viewpoint of representative democracy, the basic question concerns the effect of the captain's activities on the processes of local government. There may very well be cases in which it is essential that the captain interpret the laws to the less educated and fortunate citizens, or that he intercede when his client is placed at a disadvantage by some governmental agent, and even that he interfere in the functions of government in his constituents' interest. When such interference breeds corruption, inefficiency, and a weakened morale among the executives of the local government, it cannot be considered an unmitigated blessing.

7. ELECTIONS FOR PROFIT

THE FINAL TEST FOR ALL LOCAL FUNCTIONARIES COMES ON election day. The primary and the election are "days of reckoning"; rivalry is intense, and the fight is "to a finish." This is not to be wondered at; in this sampling of precinct captains, approximately 70 per cent were job-holders with their bread and butter at stake on election day.

In preparation for election day, the captains in every part of the city try to control the elective machinery by having their henchmen appointed as judges or clerks of election. The opportunity to do this comes indirectly.* The City Election Law provided in 1928 that the county judge appoint a board of three election commissioners representing the two leading political parties, who, at least 60 days prior to an election choose three electors as judges and two as clerks of election for each precinct in the city. The members of the local election boards have to be residents of the area they represent and are divided equally between the two parties. In view of the many precincts in the city and the partisan character of the Board of Election Commission-

* Citizen's Association of Chicago, *New Election Law Needed*, Bulletin No. 75 (1928), p. 4. Statement by JUDGE E. I. JARECKI, of the Cook County Court:
"There are more than 12,000 judges and clerks of election appointed by the Board of Election Commissioners and confirmed by the County Judge, but every one of them must be chosen from lists of persons affiliated with the majority or minority party—Democratic or Republican. Under that peculiar provision of our election law . . . it has been the custom, an almost unavoidable one, to select such local election officials from the lists of applicants recommended by the managing committees and ward leaders of each party. The curse of Chicago elections is the method prescribed by the Illinois election law for selecting judges and clerks—and its limitations."

ers, it has become the custom to delegate the selection of the local election officials to the precinct executives.

The procedure followed by the precinct captain was to choose the men and women he desired as election officials in his area, then to submit the list to the ward executive who, in turn, conveyed these lists to the Board of Election Commissioners. The board, after such wrangling for factional control, notified the applicants to appear for an examination, usually consisting of filling out blanks. Appointment followed soon afterwards.

The political party represented by the minority member of the board of election commissioners received two judges and one clerk in each odd-numbered precinct; the party having a majority of members on the board received two judges and one clerk in each even-numbered precinct. The election officials were paid $7 a day for primaries and elections, $5 a day for registration and revision; presidential primaries and elections counted for two days' service. Similarly the precinct captain of the party in power helped to choose the polling place. It was the official duty of the Board of Election Commissioners to investigate and approve the choice, but frequently this was not done. These two privileges were guarded tenaciously by the captain in most sections of the City. In the poorer areas the ward committeeman could not even appoint his own sister, or choose his brother's shop as a polling place, without the permission of the captain of that locality.

Frequently, the election officials were directly related to the captain by blood or marriage. On many occasions the best "heelers," or adults in families likely to produce many votes, were given the posts. These officials could be depended upon for their own votes and for their implicit obedience to the precinct captain.

After the precinct election board was chosen, the captain took a direct and personal interest in getting his constituents registered. He avoided the voters in his locality who had different political affiliations, unless he saw a likelihood of swinging them to his side. He worked quietly, in order not to alarm his opponents. The city election law provided that the local election boards meet in their precincts to register the voters before the congressional election. Persons qualified to register must be citizens of the United States, 21 years or over, who have resided in the state a year, in the county 90 days, and in the precinct 30 days before an election. After registration the clerks canvass the precinct to verify the accuracy of the registration with respect to residence in the area and for other facts. Doubtful cases were notified to appear for a hearing before the local board, with further redress in the County Court and before a special county judge responsible for elections. The registry is public property, held in custody by the Board of Election Commissioners.

The manner in which the registration laws were administered varied with the zeal of the local election officials and with the power of the captains. In the first-class precincts, the election officials usually performed their registration duties in exemplary fashion. In the middle-class and poor areas, they functioned less carefully, especially where factional strife was intense or where the captains were job-holders. In some middle-class and poor areas, the captains encouraged persons who no longer lived in the precinct to register there. This was the practice more particularly of party agents who were building up new localities or were tenaciously holding on to slowly changing ones. The registration regulations were most often flouted in poor and transient areas. Some captains, in collusion with the local election boards situated in the "river" wards, where the population was congested and constantly changing, encouraged the registration of disqualified voters by colonization of the homeless and of undesirables. The official paid the voter's rent in order to hold him in the locality.

Sometimes 15 or 20 adults lived together in a dilapidated shack and used it as their legal residence. In some of the "flophouses" situated in "Hobohemia," the clerks in charge were guaranteed a reward for housing the unfortunates who later were used as voters by the precinct captain. According to numerous investigations, most election frauds emanate from these areas. Another misdemeanor discovered among the election officials in the poor areas was padding the registry with names of disqualified or non-resident voters sent to them by the captain, in order to enable "floaters" and "repeaters" to function on primary or election day without being discovered. In one West Side precinct, the election judge, later a captain, said that he found a hundred names on the books before registration began. He questioned the judge of the opposite party and was blandly informed that the names were fictitious. He was about to clear them from the books, but was promised half the names for his party if he left them as they were. They remained on the registry.

Although the law stipulated that the election clerks canvass their districts after registration, this was rarely done. The task was unpleasant and, unless encouraged by their captains, the clerks were disinclined to make the effort. One election clerk in a West Side precinct acknowledged that he had not canvassed his precinct during the six years he had had the job. Sometimes the election officials deliberately failed to send notices to voters hostile to the machine, anticipating that such voters might thus be deprived of their voting privilege.

Registration is only part of the elective process. After the party officials had assured themselves of some control of the election officials, they laid their plans to gain control of the primary vote. The primary vote was the direct gauge of the machine's power, and political agents naturally interested themselves in it more than ordinary citizens. Except for this factor, the me chanics of administering both the primary and the election were the same, and they therefore will be discussed together.

In the primary and election, the captain was at the polls before they opened. He made certain that the judges and clerks were present; that the polls books and ballots were there; that his watchers and challengers with check lists of the registered voters were ready to guard the interests of his faction. In the poor areas of the city, in violation of the general election laws, he had paid workers stationed outside the polls either to greet the voters, to electioneer, to remind, or to threaten. He had his retinue of "heelers" whom he sent to collect the delayed voters and to convey them to the polls; private automobiles or taxicabs were used for this purpose. In one instance the captain sent his lieutenant to watch the children for a mother who had promised only on this condition to cast a ballot for his ticket. Badges and circulars were also distributed by the paid workers. In some of these areas, the party agent assembled the venal voters, those whom he had given $3 to $5 to help him. In the transient areas, those to whom the captain had given "two bits" or some other "hand-out," were marshalled to "do their duty." Precinct captains in these areas stated that the most certain way of getting votes was to buy them. The amount of money allotted to them on election day by their ward committeemen was spent for exactly this purpose. The captain who was a job-holder sometimes bought votes out of his own earnings, especially when his ward committeeman or alderman was running for re-election. In first and middle-class areas, the captain telephoned, called, or sent a private car to get the dependable citizens to the polls. In all the precincts, the captains always relied on a coterie of friends and relatives for some support. They also depended upon the many voters in their districts who had received favors in the past; such people were the mainstay of their political power.

Conduct at the polls on primary and election days again varied with the locality. In the first-class residental areas and in most of the middle-class areas, the course of events was comparativly smooth. At intervals, the registered voters came to the polls. After stating their names and addresses, they received ballots initialed by one of the judges of election. They were then directed to a polling booth, where they marked their ballots which were then deposited in the ballot box. Occasionally a voter entered with a sample ballot in his hand as a guide. The situation was decidedly different in the many poor and congested areas. Again at intervals during the day, voters would appear at the polls. The captain or his lieutenant was about, list in hand, greeting and checking the voters; there was considerable noise and excitement. The voting process in some of the transient and West Side precincts was a bitter conflict in which the captain frequently stopped at nothing. Since some of the citizens in those West Side localities could neither read nor write, they lawfully sought assistance from the clerks of election. Often, however, this device was used by captains to check the reliability of the venal voter. These voters were instructed to ask for assistance so that the election official might vote for them. Sometimes the paid voter was asked to mark his ballot with a special colored lead pencil, or to tear a small piece from the ballot; the election officials of the same party were asked to be on guard. Many a fraudulent vote was marked by the captain's lieutenants for a voter later discovered to have been bedridden and most unlikely to have come to the polls. Nor did the captain's ethics preclude arrangements with one of his "floaters" or "repeaters" to cast a ballot for a voter who no longer lived in the precinct, or for a registered voter who failed to vote before the polls closed. A "floater" is an amateur, but usually homeless, a purchased voter who voted many times during the day from precinct to precinct a "repeater" is a purchased voter who voted several times in the same precinct under fictitious names, or in place of voters who failed to appear.

Another device was the "chain" or "stringing" system where the first of a string of voters was given a marked ballot to take into the polling booth to be voted. He brought out with him the blank ballot given him by the clerk which was again marked by a party worker outside of the polls and given to the next "stringer." The "stringer" was usually a petty thug who voted by force as often as he wished. In some precincts, ballots boxes were stuffed; official ballots were stolen before the polls opened, marked for a particular candidate, then returned before the count was taken. Sometimes a precinct official would threaten to throw bombs if his constituents refused to vote his way. In one instance, an open conflict ensued when two precinct officials, both intent on winning the 1928 primary, failed to reach an agreement. One was more scrupulous than his opponent and objected to the other's malpractices. A policeman was present at the polls, but he could not keep the peace because the less scrupulous official was a member of the party in power.* Stealing ballot boxes was a feature in another polling place; intimidation of election officials, substituting unscrupulous party workers for the election officials appointed by the Board of Election Commissioners, kidnapping the active party worker of the opposing faction, were other maneuvers. In one violence-ridden ward, the captain of the less notorious faction was kidnapped at six o'clock in the morning of primary day, and kept hidden until the next day. In another such ward one of the candidates for ward committeeman

---

* Chicago *Daily Tribune* (March 30, 1929): "Whenever a policeman was appealed to, witnesses said, he would turn his head the other way, so that he would not see that the Ellerites were sticking pistols in the ribs of their victims and carting them over to the election day jail at 1352 South Peoria Street, one block from the home of JudgeEmanuel Eller."

was shot down in cold blood on election day. A candidate for ward committeeman in another ward was also eliminated by gunfire, giving the candidate for this office, whose party was in power, the committeeship by default. The captains in these wards were not directly responsible; they merely followed the instructions given them by their ward committeemen.

The election officials in the poor residential areas, especially in the notorious river wards, were invariably in collusion with the precinct captains. Just as they were instrumental in assisting in illegal registrations, they helped in the various forms of fraudulent voting. The 27th Ward had a special group of ballot weighers, plain and fancy "floaters," short pencil experts, and many gunmen and kidnappers. In full view of the election officials, a captain in the "bloody twentieth" copied the names and addresses from a heavily padded registry on forms provided by his party. At intervals he sent "runners" to distribute these among the venal voters and petty thugs he had stationed near by. Soon afterwards, the polling place became filled with men and women carrying the forms in their hands. As they asked for a ballot, they read the name and address from the form. One runner had carelessly given a leaflet bearing an Irish name to a Jew; the election officials appeared to be totally oblivious to the incongruity. The election clerks assisting illiterate voters frequently marked the ballots to their own liking. This form of trickery accounted in part for the unanimity among the voters in this same ward, where the population is a miscellany of many nationalities and includes many illiterates among the voters. The election judges in many fraud-ridden precincts frequently failed to initial ballots, and thus invalidated them.

When the polling booth was closed, the captain or his special aides remained within, usually to protect the election officials who then held sway over the ballots.*   The election judges unfolded and counted the ballots; the clerks recorded and tallied.   All the election officials were legally responsible for conveying the ballots safely to the central office.   While straightening ballots, a judge of election in one of the city precincts "short pencilled" all suitable ballots, i.e., he filled in crosses opposite the names left blank by the voter, using a pencil stub so short that it could not be seen. The "short pencilling" judge performed this feat in a polling place located in a tailor shop.   Two policemen and several plain-clothesmen were present.   Also present were the captain, related to the pencil expert, a number of his aides armed with guns, and an attractive red-haired girl.   The officers and the girl were playing hide and seek; one officer was trying to shield her from the other, who insisted that she leave the polling place.   While this was going on and attention was focussed on this three-cornered drama, the judge quietly spread the ballots on a side table and marked them fraudulently.   This went on for fully five minutes before it was detected by one of the officials, and soon afterwards the judge was arrested.

In the same precinct, just before the polls were closed, two hoodlums had staged a "fight."   In the confusion the registry was stolen.   All the officials were arrested.   They were indicted by a special Grand Jury and placed on bond.   The captains quietly manipulated their release; one of the captains was a Municipal Court judge, the other was boiler inspector at the city hall.

Election officials in all localities of the city sometimes made

* Chicago *Daily News* (March 16, 1929). "BARREL BREEDS VOTES: According to the testimony by the prosecution, the fake ballots were concealed in the barrel and later when it was found the ballot box was filled with votes it was suggested that it be emptied in the barrel.   At the close of the count it was found that there were 716 ballots in the barrel, whereas only 315 persons had actually voted.   When it was suggested that the ballots be checked with the poll book, which showed exactly the number who voted, it was found the book had disappeared from the polling place."

errors, when transposing figures to the tally sheet, or they made errors in counting. Captains in the more notorious precincts in transient or congested areas sometimes doctored totals, or made wholesale changes on the sheet of final record. This usually happened when the ward boss was particularly strong, and the captain had enough influence to effect an agreement with the officials of the opposite faction or party. Other malpractices by election officials included the substitution of the original count sheet for one marked by the captain or his lieutenants and the opening of sealed envelopes containing the ballots on their way to the office of the Board of Election Commissioners, and replacing these with false ballots marked by party workers. .

After every election for the past quarter of a century, the Chicago newspapers have reported vote frauds, irregularities, and atrocities which took place in the city. Vote recounts have been a usual occurrence.* The findings disclosed by an investigation of vote frauds were that the geographic area within which vote frauds occur is limited and can be outlined on the map of the city. The authorities over the election machinery, the county judge, the election commission, and the state's attorney's office, repeatedly carry on the same conflicts around the same legal points, arising out of duplication of function and overlapping and division of authority. The partisanship of the County Board

---

* ROBERT E. TAYLOR, Board of Election Commissioners. Chicago *Daily Tribune* (May 18, 1928): ". . . The recount was of three precincts in the Twentieth ward, three in the Twenty-fourth ward, two in the Third, and one each in the Twenty-fifth and Twenty-seventh wards.

"The old 'ring system' apparently was worked in the Twenty-seventh ward. That is the system by which one ballot is first bought or stolen. It is then marked and given to a 'stinger'—man who votes in another man's name. The 'stinger' takes the marked ballot into the polling place, obtains a clean, unmarked ballot, goes into the booth, folds the clean ballot, and puts it into his pocket, comes out, and deposits in the box the ballot marked for him in advance. Then he returns the clean ballot to the vote buyer, who repeats the operation until he has the ballot box stuffed to his satisfaction."

of Commissioners determines its action in appropriating funds for special investigations. The state's attorney usually opposes and impedes the appointment of a special prosecutor and a special grand jury to investigate election frauds. The incumbent state's attorney also tries to capture the support of the attorney general, who is in a position to take charge of as many grand juries as are sitting at any time. When a dominant party splits into factions, one of these may stimulate activity in vote fraud investigations with the hope of capturing control of the election machinery and gaining advantageous publicity. The investigation further disclosed that actual frauds which can be legally proved are committed by underlings, who refuse to testify as to the identity of their superiors and thus protect the "higher-ups." These underlings usually are sentenced for contempt of court by the county judge. When prosecution is undertaken in a criminal court, it fails in a large number of cases because of lack of evidence. The political bosses furnish the money and attorneys to fight the cases. In every investigation the most constant element is the connivance of the police at the polls, who witness and tolerate vote frauds and resist investigation by refusing to give testimony. The police defer to the politician because of his power over their jobs.

Slugging and intimidation of voters have long been a chronic complaint. Bootlegging brought the new phenomenon of the wealthy machine-gun baron, who became the political boss of the area. The 1928 primary was especially bloody in several precincts and many casualties resulted. Citizens were threatened with death, and active party workers were "taken for a ride." The reasons already suggested were the intensity of the political battle, factionalism, and the alliance between crime and politics, based on obvious mutual interests. The gangster or criminal depended upon the politician for protection of illicit activities. He had a vital interest in the success of the candidates who were well disposed toward him. The politician, on the other hand, knew how active a part underworld characters took in a primary or an election. The gangsters sought protection—the politician, votes. They found they could serve each other, and most efficiently when the person in charge of the city's prosecuting machinery was leniently disposed. Bootlegging had become a centralized and concentrated occupation, and its protection was lodged in the "higher-ups." Small misdemeanors committed by "small-timers" or by agents of these larger "bootleg" plants were subject to fixing in the precincts, where it was at the same time imperative for the political agents to produce votes. The man who depended on the local "bosslet" and, through him on the man "higher-up," was particularly concerned with helping the faction or party which protected him. The cycle sometimes began at the other end. The city "boss" felt that his power was weak in certain localities; he would then summon the criminals or gangsters who had benefited from his position. They then ushered their lieutenants into the specified areas to do necessary jobs. The Granady killing in the 20th Ward illustrated such an instance.

The captains were as a rule fully cognizant of the election frauds practiced in their areas. In the poor localities, and in those particularly known for their malpractices and casualties, the local party agent or his superior was generally the promoter of such misdemeanors, even though they were performed by hirelings. Competition and strife were intense in the business of winning elections in these areas; the consequent activities in many of the West Side and river precincts were for this reason usually predatory, sordid, and demoralized. Outside of these localities, in the middle and first-class residential areas, the precinct captains manipulated elections in a more dignified and honest way. The extent to which they influenced and controlled the election officials, and guided their constituents in elections, depended upon the type of constituency they served. Frauds of a malicious type existed far less, often not at all, in the better areas.

IT IS safe to say that in Chicago the political machines control elections. Party agents are concerned far more with gains and victories for their party and with their own security, than with the maintenance of election machinery for the expression of public opinion. The party machine in control dictates the "ways and means" to a public which is either uninformed, overburdened with the activities of an urban community and the many candidates to be elected, or so apathetic as not to care about abuses that threaten the very basis of democracy.

It is clear that the ills in the registration and election machinery of the city are caused by the degradation of its personnel and administration through spoils politics. The most important practical steps toward its improvement lie, perhaps, in providing for a single election commissioner, or in placing the administration of election matters in the hands of one of the regular officers of the city or county. The elimination of all bipartisanship on the central and local election boards is also essential, since the corrupt machine frequently controls the election officials of both major parties. The requirement that precinct election officials must reside in the precinct should be abrogated. The power and responsibility for the administration of registration and election should be centered in a chief officer. The introduction of voting machines would also reduce the need for handling ballots and the frauds resulting therefrom. The captain's power is weakened by efficient administration of any local department of government; it would be especially weakened if he were deprived of power over the local election officials.

8. THE CITIZEN AND THE PRECINCT CAPTAIN

TO INTERPRET THE ROLE OF THE PRECINCT CAPTAIN IN AN urban community presupposes an understanding of the modern city. Chicago is made up of at least fifteen important national groups, located in distinctly different sections of the city. The individual citizen is occupied only in his leisure time with political activity; if it becomes burdensome, he ignores or neglects it. The complexity of the citizen's life, his political inertia, the specialization of governmental administration, the want of clearly defined party issues, the many elective offices, and the frequent elections, the rich rewards accompanying elections, are cumulatively responsible for the perpetuation of the captain and the political machine.

The local functionary is a member of a political group whose behavior is economic and psychological. The economic behavior of his group is no different from that of other economic groups in the cultural setting. The machine, just as other professions and trades, has its mysteries, codes, and standards of conduct. The persons who are part of it have a vested interest in it and the environment which sustains it.

Just as in other groups, power and fear are concomitants of the political machine. In a democracy, political power is expressed through some form of consent. It is with the manipulation of this consent that the party agent is most concerned. As in any power group, the principles include respect for government, obedience, sacrifice, monopoly of legality. Among the shames are violence, cruelty, terror, arrogance, hypocrisy, deceit, intrigue, corruption, and privilege. These are as clearly seen in the local machine as in the national party. All along the political hierarchy, it is power that is dominant. Nor is such power offensive to the other groups within the cosmopolitan community, where the myriad groups interact on each other's standards, mores, and symbols. Just so long as no dominant group is excessively offended, the group survives. Friction arises only when one political machine wishes to take power from another, or when a controlling group fails to obtain the privileges it seeks.

Administrative officials selected under this system are not under the direction of their administrative superior, but of the political sponsor by whom they were appointed and by whom they may be promoted or demoted. When the head of a department suspends a party worker, the worker turns to the captain, and he to the ward committeeman; if necessary, the city boss may be appealed to. In the end, the party worker is brought back to the department.

The Civil Service Commission is not separated from these intrigues. Promotion, demotion, dismissal, and discipline are the more drastic methods of maintaining morale; but under spoils politics, party inefficiency and conspicuous public inefficiency are the only causes for action. Faithfulness to the group and ability to "deliver" are the great desiderata. There is, however, no social discrimination because of color, race, or class; all elements of the party are given their share of jobs..

Such substitution of party for public service produces disastrous results in public administration and even in local parties. It has a fatal tendency to destroy continuity of tenure or reasonable certainty of reward for meritorious service. The party worker never knows when factional or party defeat, or the mere whim of his political chief, may cause the loss of his job. Little wonder that under such conditions, slackness, favoritism, inefficiency, and graft develop.

Among the remedies for this condition might be suggested a

salaried city manager responsible to an elected council and the public for the administration of municipal affairs. A nonpartisan Civil Service Commission, and the development of professional organization and standards among such groups as accountants and engineers engaged in the public service, will do much to strengthen morale. The development of trade unions would strengthen the power of those under civil service. The financing of political factions in local governments by funds subscribed by each member will eliminate the present system of "underground" payment of party workers from public funds.

Simple as these remedies may seem, their execution is hamstrung by the habits and methods of the political parties. One of the great problems of American democracy is the financing of its political parties. This applies as truly to municipal factions as it does to the national parties. Under the prevailing system of popular elections, thousands and even millions of voters must be reached through the press, meetings, radio, and, what concerns us most, party workers. The expense is enormous; the money must come from somewhere.

The party machine is made up of job-holders deriving a livelihood from politics. When party funds are low, these officials are assessed to supply a portion of party revenue. Contributors were invited to sign a card saying they had "willingly donated" these sums to the Illinois Republican Fund. Local machines are further sustained from within by "rake-offs" from appointed or elected officials handling public funds. Large sums, leaving much room for dishonest management, are appropriated for harbors, school buildings, parks, and highways. In the letting of contracts, high bids may be accepted, on condition that the surplus go to the party chest. The party arbitrarily assesses candidates for campaign expenditures. The amount depends upon numerous factors; the importance of the office sought, the candidate's liberality and financial resources, whether the nomination is of his seeking or imposed upon him by party strategy, and the severity of the competition. The Reed Committee investigating the expenditures of the two senatorial candidates from Illinois, William B. McKinley and Colonel F. L. Smith, in the 1926 and 1928 primary campaigns, found that Mr. McKinley expended more than $514,143 in his 1926 primary; Colonel Smith's total campaign costs were $458,782. More than 60 per cent of the funds collected by the Illinois Central Committee in 1928 came from assessments upon candidates. A number of ward committeemen in the Chicago primary of 1928 admitted contributing from $1,500 to $2,000 during that campaign.

The party secures generous contributions from wealthy men who desire some post such as cabinet office or an ambassadorship. A more insidious source of party funds is the business man or the public utility magnate who unscrupulously distributes money in order to gain special privilege. The contributions of the Insull interests in the 1926 campaign were made to a United States senator, a national committeeman, a governor of the state, a state's attorney, a mayor who was also boss of his faction, and a city boss of the party not in power. The funds contributed, in short, reached the pockets of the officers of the existing party factions in the city, county, state, and nation.

Another source of funds, especially in large cities, is the criminal element concerned with having penalties "fixed" or protection guaranteed. In the mayoralty campaign of 1927 Al Capone is alleged to have contributed $250,000 to the fund of William Hale Thompson; the latter's opponent, William E. Dever, was known to have refused an offer of $100,000 from underworld interests. "Diamond Joe" Esposito, committeeman of the 26th Ward, died at the hands of a group of beer-runners who failed to get the "protection" they expected as a result of the contributions made through him to former Senator Deneen's campaign fund. The secrecy accompanying such donations, and the numerous hands through which they pass, make any estimate of total amounts very difficult.

B., a precinct captain and bootlegger, made generous contributions to the local ward chest. His political office gave him power over the other bootleggers in his precinct, and he frequently shared in the "take." The Wickersham Committee reported the close connection between local political and criminal organizations, and further demonstrated that campaign funds are procured from what amounts to licensed violations of the law.

The job-holder, the candidate, the glory-seeker, and the criminal represent the more generous section of that indefinite public which supports the party, but they are by no means its only mainstay. Many of its members bear a hereditary or sympathetic allegiance to it and make generous contributions. However, the party cannot count on them. Neither of the two major parties is financed by dues-paying members. The funds derived from public meetings or literature are very small.

The type of workers usually engaged in a campaign are canvassers, party challengers, and, in the more notorious areas, impersonators and ballot-treaters. Homer Galpin testified that in the Illinois primary of 1926, the Crowe-Barrett organization in Cook County allowed not less than $25 per precinct for watchers; that in one ward they spent $7,000; and that about $70,000 was spent in the county as a whole. One-third of the expenditure of the Deneen faction in Cook County was for watchers. The captains interviewed reported that they were allotted from $25 to $80 a precinct during the 1928 primary. Assuming they received only $25, Chicago's cost for that primary on this one item was about $75,000. This does not include the cost to the city of the

30 and 60 day appointments in the various administrative offices of the local governments, or the amounts spent on publicity.

The funds received by the party in any municipality are spent on items already mentioned—the maintenance of headquarters, publicity, and workers. Party workers are used chiefly during campaigns. The agents of the machine, the ward committeemen and the captains, are actively engaged in politics throughout the year. The ward executives are allotted as much of the campaign fund as their strategic position and power demand. They apportion the money among their captains on the same basis. The captain uses his appropriation to compensate the workers in his locality. Sometimes the ward boss employs "strong-arm" workers for the entire ward.

Much of the money distributed on election day never appears in the sworn reports of the campaign managers. But taking the reports for what they are worth, it is evident that from one-quarter to one-third of the total expenditure in a campaign goes to pay party workers. Some of these perform legitimate functions; many of them give no service except their votes. This kind of virtual bribery may be more palatable to those concerned than cruder forms, but the effect upon the electoral system is equally demoralizing. A venal class of voters is created, and the essence of democracy is destroyed. The core of the problem is party financing.

We are approaching the point where a political group must either limit the effectiveness of its campaign by relying entirely on the small amount of money collected from the rank and file, or it must compromise with business interests, assess office-holders, make heavy demands upon candidates, or steal from public funds. If the decisive factor in campaigns is money, if that money flows from selfish interests instead of from the rank and file of the electorate, if it is used to corrupt the electorate or its representatives, we have not yet reached the goal of democracy. Corruption of elections means the vitiation and ultimate destruction of representative government.

It is not in the United States alone that political parties are financed by such questionable means. In England, financial contributions have won many individuals their candidature or a place on the King's Birthday Honors List; yet Great Britain has dealt with election abuses more effectively than any other country. The Corrupt and Illegal Practices Prevention Act of 1883 was drawn to put an end to corruption and other abuses. It has furnished a model for subsequent legislation in the United States and in other countries. The important features of British legislation on corrupt practices are the focussing of responsibility upon the candidate, emphasis on self-interest as a motive in enforcement, limitation of the candidate's expenses, and banning of contributions by those interested.

The regulation of elections in the United States is largely a state function. Congress may regulate the "time, place, and manner" of the election of national representatives and senators, and it may "make all laws which shall be necessary and proper for carrying into execution the foregoing powers, and all other powers vested by this Constitution in the government of the United States, or in any department or officer thereof." However, within the broad limits of the Fourteenth, Fifteenth, and Nineteenth amendments, the states fix the qualifications for participating in national elections, and regulate the machinery of casting, counting, and certifying the votes. The power of Congress is indisputable in the conduct of congressional elections. The Newberry decision left in doubt the whole question of congressional control of primary elections, nor have subsequent decisions cleared up the question as to congressional power over primaries.

THE CITIZEN AND THE PRECINCT CAPTAIN

The corrupt practices law of 1925, which is our basic law, applies only to final elections, omitting primaries and conventions. It regulates campaign contributions to candidates or national committees; excepts expressly the state and local committees. and aims to secure continuous publicity about receipts and expenditures. The treasurers of political committees must file regular reports four times a year, with additional reports during campaigns between the tenth and fifteenth days, and on the fifth day next preceding the date of the general election. All statements of committees must be preserved for two years from date of filing.

An outstanding defect of the act, as already indicated, is its failure to include the regulation of primaries, which are dependent for control on congressional investigation, and for punishment upon legislative disbarment. The act fails also to prescribe uniform committee reports and accounting methods for both contributions and expenditures; contributions from "non-party" organizations need not be accounted for. A serious defect is that the national committee of the party is held responsible for expenditures, not the individual candidate. The act fails, furthermore, to include the expenditures of the state, county, ward, and precinct committees. For the act to be really effective, it would have to include a more penetrating analysis of contributions and their sources, a centralization of responsibility, and provision for more adequate enforcement.

The state is better able to deal with malpractices in primaries and final elections than the national government. The state may limit the expenditures of candidates for senator and representative. It may regulate primary election expenditure, and control the state and local committees. Candidates are subject to its control. In fact, the only agencies beyond its control are national committees operating across state lines. State legislation is di-

rected generally against corrupt expenditures, treating, person-
ation, contributions to two opposing candidates, and political
committees.

Except perhaps for Massachusetts and Wisconsin, the results
of state legislation have in most instances been discouraging. The
Illinois law specifically prohibits solicitation of contributions
from members of the classified civil service, but does not otherwise regulate campaign funds. During the reign of the Thompson machine, this prohibition was flouted, and it was generally
known that Thompson's "men" in public service paid to the party
funds sums proportionate to their earnings.

Publicity, usually after a primary or an election, is the method used to control campaign funds in the United States. In the
regulation of campaign funds, the expenditures of others than
the candidate are very difficult to regulate, unless some such plan
is adopted as in the Massachusetts statute. This law permits the
candidate to select an agent, but holds the candidate responsible
for all the acts of the agent and for all reports. Money may be
spent only by the candidate, his agent, or by the political committees. The law specifies that a political committee is the regularly elected party committee and any other group of five persons
associated for political purposes. The names of the committee
treasurer and of the political agent must be filed with the secretary of state. The Minnesota law is exemplary in its provisions
forbidding any person to solicit from any candidate on behalf of
any charitable or religious organization or philanthropy, or to
invite him to subscribe to a social or entertainment club of which
he is not a member.

The attention of legislators has generally been centered on the
regulation of expenditures, not on the control of contributions.
The most widespread regulation is that directed toward bribery.
This refers not only to the direct purchase of votes, but also to the

use of any material compensation to influence the electorate. Yet there is little accord as to which practices are illegal. Money spent for refreshments "not including intoxicating liquors, but including cigars and tobacco," Massachusetts regards as legitimate expenditure. Hiring conveyances to transport voters to the polls is still legitimate practice in most of the states. The actual hiring of workers on election day, including the number of watchers and challengers, is unregulated in Illinois, whereas Wisconsin prohibits the employment of election-day workers without exception, but does not legislate against electioneering.

Although publicity throws light on the practices detrimental to legitimate election methods, it does not in itself remove the evil. The offenders must be punished and prevented from engaging in illegal practices. At the present time, Illinois and Chicago mete out punishment through criminal procedure; the prosecuting attorney institutes the proceeding, the grand jury indicts, and the petty jury convicts. This task is extremely cumbersome. Many states substitute for this method vote contest procedure, even though it can be instituted only against the successful candidates.

Contests over legislative offices are decided in the body to which a candidate has been elected. Illinois and most other states depend for enforcement exclusively on ordinary criminal procedure and on contest procedure. Massachusetts has improved upon this method by introducing less formal proceedings to bring to light infractions of the law as bases for subsequent prosecutions. These are known as the "inquest," the audit, and the summary.

The means for improving popular government under our present bi-party system lies in providing enforceable state laws requiring adequate publicity for party income, as to source, amounts, and distribution at primaries and elections; in aiding the poorer candidates from the public treasury; in close adherence to a thoroughgoing merit system; and in setting up adequate machinery for the regulation of primaries and elections. The party agent in the smallest units would be definitely influenced by such changes.

With the propaganda techniques used by the captain there is no quarrel. Disregarding for the moment motives, rewards, and corrupt practices, the captain is indispensable to present-day American ballot-box democracy. The drudgery involved in canvassing, entertaining, and persuading an apathetic public to vote is sufficient to entitle him to some reward. The question is what it should be and from what source it should come. The other activities he performs, particularly his intervention in the agencies of government, and his election day malpractices, must be disapproved. His charitable deeds, as has been pointed out, are of a kind more legitimately left to the jurisdiction of the trained social worker.

It cannot be repeated too often, however, that the power and activities of the local agent are conditioned by the tone of the entire party system. If the captain can "fix," it means that some member of his party is there to assist him—"fixing" involves a vast ramification of power. The morale of the general electorate also influences the captain's activities. If governmental agencies, judicial or administrative, are inefficient, harsh or informal, the busy or uninformed citizen seeks aid from some neighbor who can furnish it. That this useful neighbor makes a profession of doing just such favors does not impair his usefulness to the troubled citizen who is willing to give his vote in return. This vicious circle strikes at the basis of political democracy; it destroys intelligent, independent citizenship. Tightening the loopholes in the judicial and administrative agencies, providing better trained and more humane personnel, removing party power over elected officials, and placing responsibility upon fewer men are some of the moderate changes which may improve the present pathological situation.

WHAT TANGIBLE means may be used, then, to bring about a working political democracy in a large metropolis? The outstanding defects at present are spoils politics, which permeates the entire party system; corrupt elections; and the conflicting mores of a citizenry lacking any focal interest in government, except perhaps during a crisis.

To hold the local factotum in the role of party agent and mobilizer of public opinion, some constructive steps are: to devise new methods of financing the political parties; to place the organization and election management in the precinct upon a non-professional, unsalaried basis; to create a fund for a few efficient party secretaries or managers, by assessment upon members and sympathizers; to promote laws against corrupt election practices. Under such a dispensation, the political machine would gradually cease to exist, for there would be no need to make political appointments in order to maintain an effective working organization, nor would the temptation be so great to accept rewards for special favors in order to swell the party purse.

The machine is satisfied with its present position and power. If any changes are to be effected, they will have to be initiated by public-spirited citizens outside the political parties, which are now so submerged in machine methods that it is difficult to think of the one without the other. Cincinnati has become one of the best governed cities in the United States through the City Charter Committee, a group of interested and daring citizens who revolted against the machines of both parties, and formed a voluntary unit concerned with organizing the precincts for clean government.

It is believed by some authorities that the spoils system in the larger American cities is a result of the wide discrepancies between political power and distributed wealth. If a few men own most of the wealth, while the many hold most of the votes, bargaining and corruption necessarily ensue, unless those who have the votes intend to use them to improve their collective existence. Otherwise those who have wealth and seek political power, or who seek more wealth or privilege through this power, inevitably use their dollars to gain their ends. The hungry man who has no bread forgets his principles and sells his vote if there is a market for it; the urban bosses and their factions are the entrepreneurs in this bartering. If the more conscientious citizens were moved to provide for the "forgotten man," and at the same time to enact local laws limiting the amount of money to be spent on elections, and to enforce these laws if they were willing to give a tithe of their earnings for the maintenance of their party, the power of wealth would be reduced immeasurably, and the spoils system abolished.

That the local party is a part of the general election machinery is recognized by the various statutes regulating party procedure. The decentralized, bipartisan administration of elections gives the captain control over the election officials and a chance to defraud the electorate of its votes. The many small voting areas or precincts in Chicago overburden the local party with innumerable agents. If the voting areas were enlarged, the number of officials in charge would then be decreased and the party would need fewer agents. The payment of their salaries might then be derived directly from party coffers—not, as now, indirectly from the public treasury. An interested public could make itself heard in an area larger than the precinct, if it so desired. Insofar as the actual mechanics of an election are concerned, efficient officials in the local polling places, apportioned according to the number of voters in the area, would not find the task very difficult.

The apathy of the urban voter during normal times may be overcome by making voting less time-consuming and tedious, and by clarifying issues. An amendment calling for a constitutional convention to provide for the short ballot, for less frequent elections, and for direct popular election of the President (as an aid to distinguishing local from national issues) are some devices toward that end.

The captain is an indispensable appendage of the political party. His work as community agent will continue as long as the voters require it. It will be restricted whenever the merit system is stringently applied to the administrative agencies of the city, whenever his power to exchange favors with political friends in these agencies is curtailed, and whenever money is regulated, or is entirely divorced from elections. With the diversity of standards in the city, the "small fry" of the party hierarchy, concerned with nominations, elections, and the control of public opinion, remains in the precarious position of mollifying or straddling the issues of the dominant groups in order to get majority consent on relevant common acceptances. The heterogeneity of standards within the cosmopolitan area is thus, perhaps, one reason for the continuance of the party machine.

Perhaps, in the process of living together, the citizens of American urban democracy will themselves maintain a continuing interest in government, will cease to depend on the interpreting, adjusting, and intermediating functions of the party agent, and will choose their representatives and settle their differences on the basis of common understanding and more clearly defined standards. Perhaps the need for living together humanely and constructively will bring about the structural and administrative changes necessary for a truly democratic city, and then the role of the political party and the precinct captain will be altered beyond prediction.